MAKING A HOUSE YOUR HOME

-DEDICATION-

For my father, Michael Charles Nolan,
who is my rock, mentor
and inspiration.

MAKING A HOUSE YOUR HOME

The Essential Guide to Modern Day Homemaking

Clare Nolan

Lifestyle Editor, YOU Magazine

KYLE BOOKS

First published in Great Britain in 2011 by
Kyle Books
An imprint of Kyle Cathie Limited
192–198 Vauxhall Bridge Road
London SW1V 1DX
general.enquiries@kylebooks.com
www.kylebooks.com

10 9 8 7 6 5

ISBN: 978-0-85783-062-3

Editor: Judith Hannam
Project editor: Hilary Mandleberg
Copy editors: Juliette Tomlinson
and Sarah Stewart Smith
Designer: Dale Walker
Picture research: Clare Nolan
Photography: Clare Nolan
(except for photos listed on
pages 285–286)
Editorial assistant: Laura Foster
Proofreader: Kathy Steer
Production: David Hearn
and Nic Jones

A Cataloguing In Publication
record for this title is available
from the British Library.

Colour reproduction by ALTA
London

Printed and bound in China by
C&C Offset Printing Co., Ltd.

CONTENTS

A home is not merely a collection of furniture, or a study in taupe. It is not a perfect echo from a magazine spread. It is more than paint charts, swatches and the shallow preoccupation with beauty over reality. Yet neither is a home just the sum of our functions; it is has to be more to us than the dirty pots and pans, the toilet brushes, the laundry piles, the ignored leaflets on the doormat. So what marries these two aspects, what softens the lines between the form and the function of the home?

This isn't just another coffee table book about making your home 'look the part' or showing you how to follow the latest interiors trends. It's a book that will help you create the very best version of your home for you – a home that not only supports you, but is one in which you and your family will thrive. It's about the small things that you think might not matter, as well as the big things that definitely do and the everyday bits in between that get lost along the way.

We invest so much time, money and emotion in our homes. Family rituals and a lifetime's memories are centred around them, from the everyday to the major milestones and the rites of passage. Home acts as an anchor, a constant – the items we chose to place within it are the backdrop for our day-to-day lives. How you select and choose what goes into your home, and how you decide to piece it all together shapes your everyday experience and can have a direct impact on your enjoyment and happiness.

I know how much home matters because I've seen the ferocity of emotion with which people react when things go wrong. Home really does matter. Getting it right so that it works for you, supports you, reflects who you are, is absolutely central to your happiness. The good news is that it's totally within your capabilities to improve your home. I passionately believe that everyone has the necessary skills to make their home a happier, more beautiful place to be. I'll help you to breathe life and vitality into it – to help provide comfort and give you a smile.

In this book, I've laid my home bare for you, so, alongside the glossy and glamorous images of all the aspirational spaces that have inspired me and given me ideas to use myself, you'll also see photos of my home too. You'll see behind closed doors – into my daily life – inside my kitchen cupboards as they really are; how I make a bedroom welcoming for friends when they come to stay; the simple things I do to make the everyday special. I'll show you many of the tips and secrets I've learnt over the years, simple, but useful and practical ideas from my home to yours, from someone who's just as busy with life, love, work and family as you are.

Working within the lifestyle magazine industry for nearly fifteen years as an interiors writer, stylist and editor has meant that I've met some of most talented and inspirational people in the business, from design icons at the height of their career to fledgling up and coming designers and makers straight out of college. I've had access to the most incredible homes, places and products, and have spent a huge portion of my working day, week in week out, searching out the best products. I've sat on the sofas, sniffed the candles, poured over the fabric and wallpaper samples. This book is a chance for me to share all those nuggets of information, so that you can shop, style and think like a pro yourself.

Piecing together a home is an ever-evolving process. Things come and go (mostly come, if you're a hoarder like me). It's an ever-changing masterpiece of your creation and should reflect your tastes, experiences and needs. In Chapter One, Getting the Basics Right, I'll help you discover the right rhythm and theme for your home to fit the way you live, and the way you want to live. Also to find a signature style that fits your inner style-blueprint and a colour palette that will make your heart sing.

Yes, there are more exciting things to life than cleaning, but there is something dignified, worthy and honest in keeping an orderly home. In Chapter Two, Chaos to Calm, I'll talk you through putting measures in place to help give your home a domestic detox and in the process enable you to gain a sense of control.

In Chapter Three, Making the Most of What You've Got, I'll show you the potential in the items you have, to avoid the knee-jerk reaction of chucking out the old and buying new. There's pleasure to be had from 'playing', or moving things around – sprucing up and re-evaluating what you already own and putting it in the right place.

Shopping is a skill and considered, careful shopping is an art that everyone can learn. I've learnt to be a professional shopper through my work as a magazine editor and stylist. I've trawled the shops, boutiques and trade shows for the best products; it has trained my eye to discern the difference between well made and not, beautifully conceived and designed, or not. In Chapter Four, Be a More Considered Shopper, I'll talk you through how to spot quality, how to buy for longevity, and how to shop to bring character to your home.

The 'feel', the atmosphere, the vibe, the *je ne sais quoi*; all synonyms for that elusive sense of balance and completeness. In Chapter Five, Getting the Feel Just Right, I explore the 'non-visuals'; aspects of homemaking that you can utilize to create a home that not only appeals to the senses and reflects the season, but one that absolutely, utterly feels like home, your home.

In the last chapter, Piecing Together The Jigsaw, I'll share my styling tricks to help you pull your home together like a pro.

GETTING THE BASICS RIGHT

Starting the process of thinking about what to do to truly make a house your home means, I believe, considering both the practical and the emotional aspects of your life.

On the practical side, think about how you live – your lifestyle. This isn't about whether you like a neutral palette or couldn't live without colour. Nor is it about loving 50s retro or only wanting to live with French-style shabby chic.

For a moment, step away from questions of style and look beyond. What is it you actually do at home? What do all the people in your home do? How do you all spend your time?

Making a house your home means ensuring that whatever you do at home, you'll enjoy doing it even more. It's to do with adding quality to the experience and providing an environment where you and your family can thrive. That means thinking not only of the things that would make your life run a little bit more smoothly (more storage, better plumbing perhaps?), but those that would make your home a happier place to be.

What changes do you need to make to your home to ensure it's supporting your lifestyle? Think not only about your current way of living, but take into account your hopes, dreams and aspirations for your future lifestyle. Think about the hobbies and interests that make you happy and try to provide for them within the home – happiness is inevitably linked to the fulfilment of our needs. Once you've worked out what's missing, draw up what I call a 'lust-list must list' of the things you feel you need and want to include in your home. It's surprising to find that, with a little ingenuity, it's possible to achieve elements of most of the things on your list, even if you're short on space.

The visual aspects of home-making also play a huge part in making home a happier place to be. If you don't get the 'feel' of your home right, you'll never love it. It's as simple as that. Every single element that we choose to bring into our home makes a difference – from the style of sofa or light fitting, to the design on a cushion cover. Even the flowers you choose and the way you arrange them in a vase contribute to the overall mood. Getting to know your likes and dislikes (and those of other family members), and developing your signature style (see page 16) is a sure-fire way of creating a home you'll feel comfortable in.

Colour too, has a huge impact on the mood of a home. It is a powerful tool and has the ability to make your heart sing or sink. One person may see an all-white space as an inspiring blank canvas, while another may perceive it as a boring soulless space with no heart. One person's energizing and uplifting vivid pink walls can be enough to bring on a migraine in someone else. It's all a matter of your personal response.

So spend time thinking about the needs and dreams of everyone in your home and take into account their preferences for colour and décor wherever possible. If you can find a way of making everyone in your household feel fulfilled within the space you have, you'll be rewarded by seeing many more smiles. That may mean including Peppa Pig or Sponge Bob somewhere, but it will be worth it.

THE DREAM
A whole wall dedicated to books. Walls lined floor-to-ceiling, wall-to-wall. Visions of a country-house library with dusty leather-bound books.

LIBRARY

A table piled with books shows off current favourites.

THE COMFORTABLE COMPROMISE
Without a whole room up for grabs, section off an area; a corner of a room or a tabletop to create a 'mini library zone'.

Make the most of every available space you have – even hallways can come in handy.

THE PRACTICAL SOLUTION
Shelves and units are less of a commitment and easier to squeeze in.

Lust-list must list

Fulfilling your needs and wants and those of your family makes for a happier home.

As I've already said, happiness is linked to the fulfilment of our needs. We all have the small pleasures that keep us ticking along, that feed our souls and that make us smile. It might be reading the newspaper in its entirety from start to finish in peace and tranquility (Jonathan, my other half) or losing yourself in the garden for ten minutes and coming back with a few scented flowers to fill a vase (me). Search out the pleasures that float your boat and make something of them or, as I always say, 'feed your needs'. If you can make the things you enjoy in life even more of a pleasure, then you're on the right track.

THE DREAM

Lists are good as they focus the mind. This is where the 'lust-list must list' comes in – 'lust' as in all the things you're lusting after, and 'must' as in the very basics that you need. Consider what makes you tick. What is key to your enjoyment? What do you lust for? Think big, as though anything is possible; this allows your mind to free itself of all the limiting realities of day-to-day life. You can come

back to reality later on in the process. Do you hanker after a fully functioning craft room, with storage for all your rolls of fabric and ribbons, jars of buttons and sequins? Would you love a cinema room with surround sound and a sofa each for all the family? How about a library with wall-to-wall shelves, a little wooden ladder and leather-bound books? Daydreaming helps define what you need from your home as well as refine your taste. You'll find it's a useful exercise in itself, even if nothing concrete ever comes out of it.

THE REALITY

Now it's time to think in terms of reality. Begin by prioritising – what's the most important thing on your list? Supposing it's that library. How much space can you dedicate to it? Is there a room that is currently unused that you could take over? Or do you need to scale your dream back a little? Would a corner of a room work as a library instead of an entire room? It's surprising what you can squeeze into a tight space when you really have to. You may not have space for that full on library, but you probably have a quiet corner somewhere with room for a chair and a few books. Add a floor lamp that casts a good light, throw a gorgeous blanket over the chair and you've got a reading corner that goes some way to fulfilling your dream.

THE COMFORTABLE COMPROMISE
A dedicated cutting patch with plenty to harvest from spring to autumn – perfection on a smaller scale.

CUTTING GARDEN

THE PRACTICAL SOLUTION
Planters filled with spring bulbs followed by annuals – just enough to feed the passion.

THE DREAM
Row upon row of seasonal scented flowers, with enough to create wild extravagant displays whenever I want – plenty to give away too.

THE COMFORTABLE COMPROMISE

The key to making your 'lust-list must list' work is to compromise but that means you need to know why you're lusting for something in the first place. If you truly want something for the simple joy it will bring (reading peacefully, say), then the finer details (the fact that you're actually in the corner of the landing and not in a library) won't hugely matter – you'll just be so glad of the peace and quiet. However, if the motivation for wanting a library isn't the reading but something else – improving the value of your property, for example – then you'll need to find another solution.

THE PRACTICAL SOLUTION

It was always my dream to have a dedicated cutting patch in my garden so I could bring fresh flowers into the house all through spring and summer. For many years that wasn't going to happen, but I nevertheless managed to squeeze enough flowers for cutting into two 90cm planters in my town garden. That compromise worked fine for me. It fed my dream.

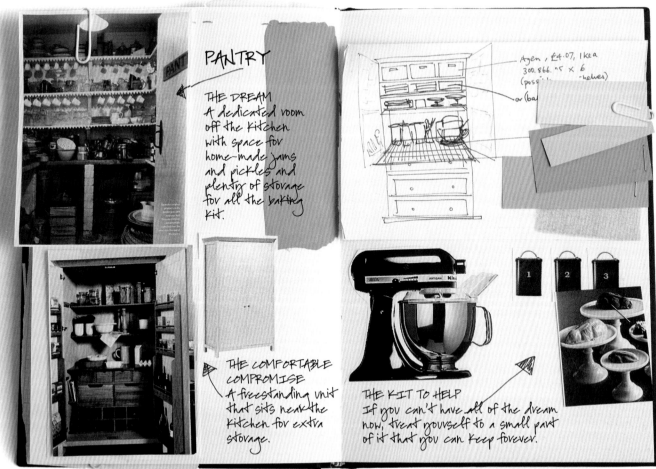

PANTRY

THE DREAM
A dedicated room off the kitchen with space for home-made jams and pickles and plenty of storage for all the baking kit.

Agen, £4.07, Ikea
300.866. 75 × 6
(poss ... -helves)
or (ba...

THE COMFORTABLE COMPROMISE
A freestanding unit that sits near the kitchen for extra storage.

THE KIT TO HELP
If you can't have all of the dream now, treat yourself to a small part of it that you can keep forever.

THE CINEMA ROOM COMPROMISE AND SOLUTION
The dream: A dedicated room with all the high-tech gadgets you would expect.
The compromise: A hide-away projector, blackout blinds or curtains, and a supersized sofa.
The practical solution: A TV upgrade which includes surround-sound speakers.
The kit to help: A popcorn maker, floor cushions and cosy throws.

THE DRESSING ROOM COMPROMISE AND SOLUTION
The dream: A walk-in wardrobe with wall-to-wall storage.
The compromise: A custom-made wardrobe built in along one wall of the room.
The practical solution: Shop-bought wardrobes customised with additional hooks and hanging racks.
The kit to help: Luxury padded hangers, pretty lavender bags and great storage boxes.

MODERNIST (see below)

You are one for pure, mid-century modern design teamed with contemporary items and modern art. The look is very restrained, but the feeling is one of ease. Antiques or ethnic items do not sit happily in this environment.

BOHEMIAN (see above)

This style is a fantastically free, youthful look with a slight hippy edge to it. It's not so much about the items in the room, but about the room's spirit. Colour and clashes of colour and style are an ingredient of bohemian style, but the heart of this look relies on your own collections and their artful display.

MINIMALIST
(see right)

You have a love of the purest and simplest light-filled spaces – generally those that have clean architectural lines combined with the colour white and with other soft, natural tones. You appoint the room with a minimum of objects, accessories and art.

TRADITIONALIST (see left)

Your bent is for a blend of old and new, mixing proper old furniture and antiques with 'fun' items. You love colour, texture and print, and filling the space with your furniture, objects, books and art. You take your lead from the grand and often slightly faded old English country houses.

Find your signature style

Your signature style is your blueprint, the path your instinct leads you along, the way you always see things. You might even call it your 'style taste buds'. Some small aspects and nuances of your signature style will probably change over time as your taste evolves and develops, but the basics will always stay the same.

Don't think you've got a particular style? Think again. There's a reason you're drawn to certain things – that battered old leather club chair rather than a brand new buttoned and tailored mohair wing chair, or that carved wooden side table rather than a lacquered cube.

Of course the choices you make are also based on certain practicalities. (Is this fabric more hardwearing than that one? Will this cupboard accommodate my stuff better than that one?). The style of your house will affect your choices too, but chances are that your house reflects your signature style anyway.

Figure out who you are

Before you start any decorating projects, take some time to examine what you like and why you like it.

WHAT FEELS RIGHT TO YOU?

If your house doesn't 'feel' right you're never going to love it. Everything that you choose to live with affects how a space feels. A neutral-looking decorating scheme with a thick-pile carpet, for example, is going to feel calming and relaxing; a scheme that includes an old industrial brick wall with exposed ironwork will have a very different feel. Have you been to a hotel or restaurant that you loved the feel of as well as the look? If you can pinpoint a few places that you're really drawn to that will help you decide what you'd like from your own space. It's simple. Just follow your heart.

WHICH STYLE FAMILY SUITS YOU BEST?

Working out which style family suits you best (see left) makes putting a scheme together easier, but be aware that there are crossovers and you might be attracted to a little of one and more of another.

WHAT DO YOU DO IN YOUR DOWN TIME?

Look at the kind of holidays you take and how you like to spend your free time. These can provide a clue to the sort of decorating scheme that will suit you.

Keep it real

Of course, there comes a moment when the dream has to be tempered by reality, as these pointers will explain.

BE PRACTICAL

Take into account your circumstances. Do you need to be really practical right now because you've got three children, even though what you desire more than anything in the world is to have that white carpet in the lounge? Remember though, there's no point buying something that you'll never be able to relaxed enough to enjoy. If necessary, it can wait.

MATCH YOUR PERSONALITY

Take into account your personality and domestic traits. For example, are you messy? If you are, then don't choose a minimalist look – it'll be far too high-maintenance for you.

THINGS CHANGE

Finally, remember that time doesn't stand still. As we grow older what we require from our homes changes, so keep checking in with yourself that your home is still what you need it to be.

Where to look for inspiration

One of the perks of my job is that I get to visit trade shows where designers and manufacturers launch their latest products. But I have to admit that it's not always a new product, a glossy mag, an interior book or a lifestyle internet site that inspires me most. The key often lies in 'real' spaces – my friends' homes, the location houses I've hired for shoots, the homes I've featured in magazines and the hotels I've stayed in over the years.

You never know what you'll find inspiring until you see it. Sometimes it's the tiniest thing that will spark an idea off in your mind and lead you on a path to something beautiful. Be aware and take notice of everything, from the leaves on the trees, the tone of pink in spring blossom and the colour of the sky, to how the curator at a gallery has framed and hung the artwork or how a stylist has put together a table setting in a shop window. Equally, when you go to a bar, restaurant or hotel, look at the way these have been styled and decorated. You'll gradually find your own taste and style emerging as the inspiration works its way into your subconscious.

Harness your ideas and make them real

Start by making a list of your ideas and putting them into some kind of order. Edit and refine your ideas while imagining the finished space. Remember to think about how you want to feel as much as how you want things to look.

I approach the execution of an idea in the home or garden in much the same way I work through the process of putting a story together for the magazine I work on. The process takes the following form:

COLLECT AND COLLATE VISUALS
Torn-out pages from magazines, photos, references from websites, any relevant visual that I love gets pasted into my sketchbook alongside my sketches. Photos of existing features that need to be taken into account, such as architectural details or large pieces of furniture that have to be part of the scheme, also get pasted in.

EDIT
Editing helps you find the 'heart' of an idea and makes it sing out with clarity. This stage is critical. Take your time to sift through and edit your choices, working with and weaving in what you want to keep from the things you already own as you go along.

RESEARCH PRODUCTS
This is the only way to track down the best items for the job at the right price. We've never been so well placed to find designer products at prices that offer exceptional value for money as we are now. The internet is key to my research – it means I can do all the legwork without actually leaving the house.

MAKE A MOODBOARD
A moodboard lets you see your choices displayed all together, giving you an at-a-glance view of your idea as it evolves. On the right is the A3 moodboard that I put together to style my open-plan lounge/diner (below). I used pins to attach the swatches so they could easily be moved around, edited out or popped in my bag and taken to the shops so I could colour-match or compare to other items.

KEEP DESIGN FILES
These help keep you tidy in both thought and execution. You'll rarely lose vital information or a useful contact.

Henley Lounge/Diner Area

Cloth House Washed GRE

Cloth House Unwashed GREY

Manor House Gray
Comforter White

Bankers glass dome

runner for stairs

George Smith
*Keeping as is.

Rhino   Slate

X 2 Wing chairs
(coverings?)

*antique 'vitrine' table, bought at auction

Pimpernel & partners

BTC

Create a personal colour palette

I believe we all have our own instinctive colour palette – a family of colours that we're drawn to because it's easy on the eye and makes us feel good. For many people it will be a palette that's safely in the neutral camp, while for others it will be one that's downright bold.

Take the time to think about colour and discover what you love. You'll know when you've found it because it will evoke an emotional response in you. A colour can and should make your heart sing. There are many ways to narrow down the colours that make up your personal colour palette.

LOOK FOR INSPIRATION EVERYWHERE

Everything and anything can inspire a successful colour combination but nature is particularly inspiring. Just the 40 or so different pinks in a single rose can be the inspiration for an all-pink-and-white room. In the same way, forest bark and lichen can be key to the perfect brown-based greys and greens you need for a super-chic modern country interior. Looking at these natural combinations will help you figure out what works together and what accent colours you can bring in successfully. Artwork is also a great way to be inspired: if colours work well together in a painting, you can be confident they'll work in your decorating scheme too.

LOOK AT YOUR CHOICE OF CLOTHES

If your wardrobe's got plenty of sequinned and other sparkly fabrics, you'll probably be a fan of metallic finishes. If you feel great wearing your scarlet dress, then red will probably work for you in your scheme (but red's a powerful colour so it's not wise to paint all four walls scarlet – instead work it in as a 'hero' accent colour in an otherwise subdued scheme). If your a wardrobe's crammed with a lot of black and brown, then look at your shoes and jewellery for clues as to which colours attract your attention. Then you'll have a starting point for a palette in reverse, for instance a white room with black and emerald accents.

LOOK CLOSELY AT THE COLOURS YOU LOVE

If you know you love white, grey, pink and green, then I suggest you find references from magazines and paint charts that show these colours together. Really look at them to see how they work together, which will work best as dominating colours and which should only be used in small doses as accents.

REVISIT THE COLOURS YOU HATE

Colour changes depending on how it's used, which is why I advise never saying, for instance, 'I hate orange' or 'I hate brown'. Instead be specific – say that it's a particular brown chair or orange sofa that you dislike. This keeps your mind open to the possibility that another item in brown or orange could be especially appealing.

*Piecing together a 3D colour palette 'moodboard' allows you to discover combinations that work together, as well as those that don't. Start by pulling together anything and everything you love – from all over – then begin to group the items into colour palettes. Play with what you think works, editing everything until you get to something to love.

How colour works

We see colour when our eyes respond to light wavelengths in the spectrum. In fact, colour is something of an illusion as the perception of colour varies from individual to individual.

THE 'FEEL' OF COLOUR

There's no need to worry about the terminology of colour – words such as 'hue', 'tone', 'shade' and 'tint'. Most people, even experts, use these words interchangeably – which makes things very confusing.

It's well-nigh impossible to set down colour rules as there are always exceptions. What matters is your response to colour and how it makes you feel. Harness your responses so you surround yourself with the colours that make your home look good and that in turn make you feel great within that space. Remember, one person's invigorating dark red walls may make another person feel overwhelmed and stressed.

THE WAY COLOUR CHANGES

Colour isn't always the same. Both natural and artificial light change it, so take this into account when making your colour choices. Form, for instance the shape of a vase, sofa or table, affect the way we perceive colour, as do texture and finish. These last two change the way light is absorbed or reflected. A glossy black floor, for instance, won't make a room as dark as you think it might; instead it will reflect light so the floor appears like the surface of a glossy, inky lake. By contrast, matt surfaces absorb light and make colour appear denser and more intense.

LIGHT AND DARK

When you're choosing the background colour for a room (usually the paint for the walls), consider the amount of light that room gets. If the room faces north, colours in it will appear 'colder' than in a south-facing room. If you want to avoid the room looking dreary on an overcast day, you may want to opt for a warmer tone of the colour you like – a grey with some warm brown in it, say.

Also, consider how the light levels change in the room throughout the day. Where are the shadows cast? Are the walls bathed in direct sun?

Lack of natural light? You have two choices – either embrace the lack and create a den-like, cosy, cocooning space by using moodier colours, or maximise the light by painting with bright, light neutrals and using reflective finishes.

Not many of us have harsh sunshine streaming through the window, but if you do, avoid white as it will make the sunshine even harsher. I once painted the walls of my south-facing garden brilliant white and realised about an hour in that it was the wrong decision. Even with sunglasses on, I was left squinting and my eyes were streaming. If bright light's the problem, opt for deeper, cooler colours such as blues and greens and avoid warm colours: they'll only make you feel hot and uncomfortable.

BIG AND SMALL

Colour can be used to trick the eye. Use pale colours – shades of white and very light grey – to 'push' the walls of a small room back and make it appear much bigger. But bear this effect in mind when choosing colours for a large space: you may find that pale shades in a large room leave you feeling exposed and cold.

Dark colours can have the opposite effect, making the walls appear to close in on you. This is good if you want to make a large space feel cosier, but avoid it if you're trying to make a space look bigger.

In a small home, using a palette of tonal colours (colours that are only slightly lighter or darker than each other) will help the space feel much bigger. As you go from one small room to the next, the boundaries of each room will seem to melt away. But try painting each room a completely different colour, and a small space will feel just that – small. (See page 24 for more ideas on how colour changes space.)

Changing a space with colour

THE WALLS

1: A pure white space can feel light, airy and more spacious that it really is. It's an ideal blank canvas, but may appear cold to many people.

2: A light neutral takes the hard edge off while still being light and airy. The contrast between the pure white woodwork highlights the architectural details.

THE WOOD-WORK

5: Choosing a colour for the skirting boards alone is certainly a style statement. It creates a 'frame' effect around the room.

6: Painting the woodwork a few shades lighter than the wall colour instead of in pure white makes the woodwork blend in more.

THE FLOOR AND CEILING

9: With the floor in a dark colour, the room appears wider. The room is 'grounded' and feels less cold.

10: A tonal floor blends with the wall colour and makes the room feel calm, warm and spacious.

3: A dark colour on all four walls can make them appear closer together. You lose some sense of space, but gain warmth and intimacy. The woodwork defines the boundaries of the room, making a small space feel even smaller, but it provides a clean, crisp edge.

4: Painting one section of a wall (a chimney breast or alcoves) or one whole wall in a strong colour creates a focal point in the room.

7: Matching the skirting boards to the dark walls makes them disappear. This can be helpful to add height to a room with low ceilings. The white floor and ceiling become an uncomfortable contrast.

8: Choosing to paint just the window frame creates a focal point in the room – just as the painted wall (4 above) does.

11: Painting the ceiling, floors and woodwork in just slightly lighter shades of the wall colour neutralises the darkest colour. The result? The room feels bigger, as if it doesn't have any boundaries, which is quite suprising for a such a dark shade.

12: A dark colour on the ceiling has the effect of lowering it. This can be very useful in rooms with extremely high ceilings where you crave a feeling of intimacy.

Bring colour into your home

You can introduce colour into your home in so many ways. The rugs or carpet, the furniture, the accessories and the decorative objects all add layers of colour. But it's the choice of wall colour that can make the most dramatic difference to a space.

The paint

The walls are the largest surface area of a room so their colour has a huge impact on the overall mood and feel. Paint is one of the quickest, easiest and cheapest ways to add colour.

HOW TO GET YOUR PAINT COLOUR JUST RIGHT

✳ Always do a patch test. Never go straight from colour chart to wall. You need to see the paint in the actual room it's going to be used for. The final colour can vary surprisingly, both compared with the chart in the shop (under harsh fluorescent lighting) and when it's wet in the tin.

✳ Paint a proper test swatch; don't just slap a small amount on the wall. The existing colour may come through and you won't get a true representation. I buy test pots and paint them onto large sheets of plain paper (wallpaper lining paper is a good choice), aiming to cover an area at least 30cm². Apply two coats or one very thick coat to get a sense of the true depth of the colour, and label the sheet straight away so you know which colour it is. Having a large colour swatch that you can move around means you can compare the colour to existing curtains, flooring or furniture with ease.

✳ Your perception of the colour will change according to where it is in the room and whether it's in shade or light. Move the swatches around to different spots to ensure you're happy with the colour at its lightest and darkest.

✳ Look at the test swatches throughout the day: as the daylight changes, the colour will change too. You will also need to see how the colour looks under artificial light, so try that out too.

✳ As well as doing patch tests for your wall colour, you should also do them for the woodwork colour. Don't gamble with the colour of your varnish, stain or wax; it's hard to rectify the colour of woodwork if it goes wrong (re-sanding isn't a quick job) and it will be painful to look at every day. To do a test, get hold of a piece of wood that's the same type or similar to that of your floor/window frame/architrave, and try out the paint/varnish/oil as you would for the wall colour. Apply the correct number of coats, as well as the varnish or wax finish, as necessary. That way you'll see exactly what colour you'll end up with.

✳ If, despite everything, the paint colour you've chosen turns out to be a little strong, all is not lost; simply tone it down by mixing it with white paint (to make what's technically called a tint). Just make sure you mix it really, really well and mix enough to do the whole room plus a little extra for any touch-ups you may need. On the opposite page you can see how the strongest colour (left column) was toned down first with equal amounts of white (middle), then with three-quarters the amount of white (right column).

✳ To store leftover paint, decant the remnants into airtight containers, label (with the paint code and the name of the room you used it in), and store in a cool dark place. Storing near-empty paint cans becomes pointless after a while as the cans rust and the paint dries and flakes, making it unusable.

Neutral doesn't mean bland

'Neutral' doesn't have to mean beige, greige or magnolia. A 'neutral' is any colour you can live with that doesn't contrast with any other colour. Your neutral can be a blue, a green – whatever colour is right for you. Whether it feels like a calm, balanced 'neutral' background or stands out as a colour all depends on the way that it's used (see page 24).

The furnishings and accessories

There is colour in everything you choose to bring into a room. Even neutral greys, creams and whites, though not 'colourful', come in a multitude of shades. Layering colour in a room brings richness and warmth and can make a room feel alive.

CONTRAST

What makes a colour stand out and appear brighter and bolder is how it relates to the colours that surround it. This is true for furnishings and accessories just as much as for the wall, floor and woodwork colours. A bright blue sofa will appear neutral in a blue room but will stand out against pure white walls. Decide on the level of contrast that you feel comfortable with as it's this contrast that sets the mood in a room. Lots of contrast equals more energy; not so much contrast equals calm. It's all based on emotion and is so, so personal, but experiment and you'll soon discover what suits you.

TEXTURE

I prefer low-contrast schemes, but without the various textures that I bring in to add interest, such schemes are in danger of becoming a bit samey. Texture also changes the feel of colour – a fur throw will look completely different to a tightly woven wool throw in the same colour. Use this knowledge to add interest to a low-contrast scheme.

LAYERS AND ACCENTS

The volume, or amount, of colour you bring into a space changes how it is perceived. In the bedroom above left, blue is layered throughout the all-white room in the form of the soft furnishings to give the impression of a blue colour scheme. By contrast, the pink chair, below left, is very definitely the highlight of the room, as it's the only element of pink.

The colour of wood

Don't overlook the fact that pieces made from wood are just as full of colour as 'coloured items'. They form part of your colour palette too. There's no such thing as a generic 'wood colour'; the range of colours in woods is huge, as is the range of colours offered by the finishes. So when you're considering wood in your space – whether it's for the floor or for a piece of furniture – think about the natural colour of the wood plus the colour effect of the stain, varnish, wax or oil that will be added.

Using furnishings and accessories in a neutral scheme

✳ Cushions, rugs, throws, runners and curtains are the most obvious way to transform a space with colour. Use them either to contrast with the main scheme or to work in a range of subtle textures in harmonising colours.

✳ Pictures, prints, posters, children's art, textiles and 3D installations like floating shelves with carefully curated treasures all bring colour to a room.

✳ Your collected objects are full of colour and texture. Use them to create mini colour stories within a room. That way their colour won't be too overpowering.

✳ Use a single piece of artwork as the key to a room, picking out some of the colours in it to use for cushions, flowers, vases and other accessories.

✳ A single piece of brightly coloured furniture can add drama to a room without overpowering it.

Bringing in pattern

Pattern and colour bring spirit to a room. Subtle, tonal patterns are as quiet and soulful as a plain neutral scheme, while bolder colours and combinations of pattern will fill your space with joyful vivacity.

When you're introducing pattern, you need to understand just how much 'noise' you can take. In the same way that even a bright bold colour can be perceived as a 'neutral' (see page 26), so it is with pattern.

THINK 'VOLUME'

Regardless of the colour, size or style of a pattern, the volume of noise it creates depends on the contrast between the background and the pattern. The most subtle patterns are those that use a contrast in texture rather than colour – a self-stripe woven into a fabric, for example, or a gloss flower printed onto a matt wallpaper. Single colour patterns like these mean that even big blousy florals or full on geometrics can be subtle and very liveable. If you want to turn up the volume, you simply turn up the contrast in the pattern.

MIXING PATTERNS

A boho look involves a mishmash of contrasting patterns in multiple colours. A more traditional scheme involves perhaps one hero pattern with a mix of medium and smaller patterns, in co-ordinating colours.

PATTERN CAN CHANGE A SPACE

Use pattern to trick the eye. Stripes draw attention to the verticals or horizontals of a space. Hang a striped wallpaper horizontally in a tall space and it will look as if the ceiling is lower. A large pattern on one wall in a small room can make the room feel bigger, while a hotspot of pattern (see opposite) leads the eye from one space to another. When choosing wallpaper with a large repeat though, watch out for patterns within the pattern. Some wallpapers make the whole wall seem to 'lean'. Ask your supplier to show you a photo of the paper on a wall.

*Using bold patterns in small doses against a plain backdrop gives the pattern a chance to breathe and become the hero in a scheme. Create pattern hotspots with curtains, rugs or accessories, or restrict the pattern to just a section of one wall.

Using pattern

❋ Wallpaper is obvious as a way of adding pattern, but on one wall or on all four?

❋ Fitted flooring is a major outlay, so you must be very sure about that pattern. If in doubt, limit the pattern to just one area – a stair runner perhaps. Rugs are safer as they are moveable and (mostly) cheaper to replace. Or try painting a pattern onto the floor. It's easy to do with patience and masking tape to ensure sharp edges.

❋ Patterns in cushions, throws, artworks and all your bits and bobs give a room an instant injection of energy. Big-ticket items are an investment, so think more carefully about these. Will you still love the pattern on those curtains, sofa or chairs in years to come? Would it be safer to compromise with patterned accessories that can be changed when you tire of them?

❋ If you're a wary of pattern, go gently. Look for double-sided cushions and throws with a plain or patterned option. Use wallpaper inside cupboards, behind shelves (see left) or to line a pendant lampshade. Use patterned fabric for a subtle piping detail on a chair.

CHAOS TO CALM

I am always hugely and happily surprised by how much better my home looks after a thorough clean and sort-through. Not only that, I feel so much better for having done it. Once, I spent a whole afternoon organising my linen cupboard, and went as far as re-ironing and even re-washing some of the items that hadn't been used for a while. It became a pleasure rather than a chore.

I glued some very pretty, leftover wallpaper to the inside back of the cupboard. The sheets and duvets were folded carefully, and the pillow cases and throws re-arranged according to size and type. The finishing touch was a mist of linen spray. At the time, my life did not feel as calm or balanced as it might have been; I was 'between houses' and nothing really felt as it should. The entire process amazed me because it gave me a sense of control that I had obviously been craving. Even though it was only the tiniest, most insignificant corner of my world and invisible to others, knowing it was perfect made me feel so much better. It also taught me to never, ever underestimate the power of a domestic detox. Undoubtedly, there are always more exciting, and certainly more important things to be doing in life; but on that day, that little bit of domestic therapy was exactly what I needed.

Taming this chaos brought calm into my home as well as to my mind. For a long time celebrating the joys of cleaning has not been particularly fashionable I know, but there is something dignified, worthy and honest in keeping an orderly home. There is value in cherishing our surroundings and it is a deeply human instinct to do so.

Use common sense and stick to your own system of organisation and therefore tidiness. Treat this as the single governing rule. With this approach, it truly becomes your natural habit to put things back in their place – which will help prevent day to day clutter from taking over. I am not referring to the artful clutter that you have chosen to live with, but the dull day to day clutter of home life that seems to swell from nowhere. My instinct tells me that the key is to edit and store: regularly have throw-out sessions and create storage where you can. There are many examples in this chapter that illustrate what can be done with the general stuff of life, so that the pieces and items you want to be able to focus on will always shine out in the space. Putting a system in place to make the process of looking after the house less burdensome and preoccupying will leave you with time and space; physically, mentally and metaphorically.

Take control of everyday clutter

Life inevitably brings clutter in its wake. Loose change and receipts, recipes torn from magazines. Post, papers waiting to be filed; those annoying little piles of paraphernalia that mysteriously multiply on the kitchen worktop or on the hall table. These small things of everyday need to be corralled, before they're out of control.

To stop clutter taking over, decide where your particular hotspots are. Dot 'paraphernalia collection points' around your home in all the places where things collect. A pretty bowl for coins and keys in the hall perhaps, or a patterned box for papers that are on their way to the kitchen. Empty these strategically placed bowls and boxes regularly so the clutter doesn't build up and become an issue yet again. If you allow yourself room for the junk until clear-out day, you won't become a slave to it.

PAPERS

Where, exactly, do all those recipes, pages torn from magazines, junk-mail letters and receipts come from? I paste my recipes into a series of sketchbooks (it's far better than buying a cookery book as the recipes are my own personal choice). These items can just as easily be filed away into pretty A4 folders. Work out your own system of filing and storing on the basis of what works for you.

Bills, receipts and other items of home admin are another matter. Again, you need to find a system that works for you, but I always advise having clearly marked folders (use attractive ones, then your home admin will feel less like a chore) and institute regular clear-outs so you can keep on top of all your paperwork.

LOOSE CHANGE

Coins can look good in their own right. When they're chucked in a pile with odd keys, screws and receipts, they become a problem. To avoid the clutter, try a cute piggy bank, or a pretty box or bowl, or a wide necked bottle or jar. Put it close to where the men in the house empty their pockets. You'll be really pleased at the speed with which your coin collection grows. Use it for a special treat.

MESSY DRAWERS

Every house seems to have a 'junk drawer'. We all need somewhere to hide a few things sometimes, just to get them out of sight. However, it becomes a problem when more than one drawer is a junk drawer. To avoid all your drawers ending up in a jumble, use drawer dividers or a series of baskets or boxes to compartmentalise and store smaller items.

Accessibility is everything. Files are easier to sift through than piles. Drawer dividers isolate the smallest things and a jar for spare buttons stops means you know exactly where they are.

Storage that's good-looking enough to have on show means you're more likely to use it. Turn plain into pretty with wallpaper or wrapping paper.

Old recipes torn from magazines and pasted into sketchbooks will quickly become a useful, usable reference.

Little by little a collection mounts; loose change becomes a 'fund' and bowls of cluttered coins a thing of the past.

SPAGHETTI-JUNCTION CABLES

Even with wireless connections, there are still many cables that have to be accommodated in some way. Hiding them completely is not always possible, but you can make the cables appear neater within your home by concealing them in a soft sleeve (available from electrical shops). I also tie cables together with twist ties to keep them in check.

THE BOTTOM OF THE LAUNDRY PILE

Do handwash that silk blouse, those cashmere bedsocks or whatever handwash-only items are lurking at the bottom of your laundry pile. They're not going to get worn if they live down there are they? Once you crack on with them, you'll find they only take minutes.

IRONING MOUNTAINS

Try and do it piecemeal so it doesn't build up. It still truly amazes me what you can achieve in ten minutes (and that doesn't just go for ironing). But whatever you do, don't forfeit a whole room by filling it with your waiting-to-be-ironed pile. I keep mine out of sight in a good-sized storage trunk in the hallway until I'm ready to tackle it.

LOST AND FOUND

Start a 'lost and found' basket or box for your family. Store all those odd bits and pieces that appear from nowhere; the odd socks that emerge from the wash, the notes, receipts and fallen-off buttons you find on the floor.

Sufficient storage = a tidy home

Either you're a hoarder or you're not. I am, but I don't like living with clutter nor with the feeling of chaos that comes of having too many things out on show. That means I need plenty of storage. Getting your storage right will help you get your house under control.

Before you start storing, think about what you can bear to part with. There's no point buying into new storage solutions if you actually don't need the stuff in the first place. De-junking and decluttering can be painful, but doing it will give you the space to breathe, to think and to allow the decorative items you own to really sing and earn their place in your home.

EDIT, EDIT, AND EDIT AGAIN

This is key. Keep only things that are of sentimental value and be brutal with everything else. Your mantra should be: 'Use it, love it or lose it'. If you really can't bear to part with something and you've got enough storage space, consider having summer and winter looks. That way you can pack things away and bring them back into use as the season changes and/or the mood takes you. Rotating items gives you much needed space and allows you to carefully choose what you showcase at any one time.

Some things are harder to reject than others. In particular, things that you bought at some expense, but which just haven't lived up to expectation. Most people hang on to their retail regrets because they feel guilty about having bought them. Every time they look at them they kick themselves yet again. This is a negative thing to do.

Instead, accept that you made a mistake and take decisive, positive action. Give the item away, sell it on eBay – whichever way you choose to dispose of it, kiss it goodbye and never think of it again. Learn from your mistakes, read Chapter 4 (see pages 82–111), which

Dual-function furniture

Use furniture that doubles as storage where you can to provide even more places to stow items away. Think chests of drawers as bedside tables, a console with drawers by the door in the hallway as handy place for keys and post, a cube with a lift-off lid in the lounge to store CDs and DVDs, a bed with drawers beneath as the ideal linen 'cupboard'.

tells you how to be a more considered shopper. Promise yourself that you'll be just that bit cleverer next time.

PLANNING YOUR STORAGE

Plan ahead before you buy. No matter how lovely the chest of drawers or how irresistible the pretty storage boxes; a house crowded with rows of drawers lined up side-by-side and with stacks of storage boxes or other storage paraphernalia will start to look like it's bulging at the seams. If you need lots of storage space, then streamlined, built-in storage (see page 41) may be the best option for you.

Think about access. How often will you need to get to the items and how easy will it be? There's a big difference between how often you need to get to the Christmas decorations and how often you want to get to your clean bed linen, so make sure you arrange things accordingly. If an item is seldom used, you could free up valuable prime storage space by moving it to another part of the house – to the attic, garage or shed if necessary.

Now you see it, now you don't

Sacrificing a whole wall to storage may seem excessive, but once fitted, you'll wonder how you ever managed without it. Opt for floor-to-ceiling and wall-to-wall storage wherever possible. This is more contemporary than storage either side of the fireplace and will make the room appear much bigger when it's been painted the same colour as the walls.

In every house I've ever done up, I've always added built-in storage. Even though I've baulked at the cost while signing the cheque, I've never regretted it. It works in any room: the lounge (for books, photo albums, CD, DVDs and the like), the bedroom (a wall of storage for clothes, shoes, belts, scarves and jewellery) and the dining room (for linens, formal flatware, platters, tureens and all your china).

UNEXPECTED PLACES FOR BUILT-INS
* Under the stairs #1. If space allows, have a cupboard that is accessed at one end via a standard-sized door. This is perfect for turning into a mini utility room: a place for the ironing board, the vacuum cleaner, the brooms and mops to live. Or it might make a mini 'boot room' for outdoor shoes, umbrellas, coats and jackets and to stow away the children's scooters.
* Under the stairs #2. How about a cupboard that is accessed from the side via a door that fits the slope of the stairs? This is particularly useful if your stairs are open-plan to another room such as the lounge or dining room. Your cupboard can provide useful storage for tablelinen, vases, cutlery, out-of-season throws and other accessories.
* In whatever alcoves and niches you've got. Here you can install bookshelves, cupboards, a hidden TV cabinet – even an office area (see pages 222–235).
* In the bathroom. Have you ever bought a tiddly bathroom cabinet, plonked it on the wall and found it only did half the storage job you needed? Instead, look around for the possibility of a floor-to-ceiling built-in with room for all the shampoos, towels and other bathroom bits and bobs.

ESSENTIAL PLANNING FOR BUILT-INS
* Take into account the existing architectural details – the architraves, skirting boards and any picture rails – when planning your design. Do you want your storage to blend in with the room (paint it the same colour as the walls) or be a stand-alone feature (paint it to match the walls)?
* What do you need to store? The height and depth of the shelves and any other configuration you need inside the piece depend on it. Measure what you want to store exactly: don't guess. You will always get it wrong.

* Think about how you open the doors. Handles can completely change the look and feel of the piece so consider them at the design stage, not as an afterthought. For a minimal look without handles, consider touch-release openings.
* Think about the hinges. You can have hinges that will allow the door to open to 180 degrees, which is perfect for a cupboard housing a desk area where you need to sit without feeling that the doors are about to close in around you.
* Think about lighting. Recessed spotlights in cabinets and strip lights under shelves all shed light just where you need it. If the storage is to stand in an area that's dimly lit or where space is tight, it's particularly useful to fit a light that switches on and off when the door is opened. Painting the inside of the cupboards will help too; if the insides are a dark colour, you won't be able to see a thing.

*Feature wall or 'hidden' storage? It's all down to the surface detail on the doors. Panelling gives a subtle architectural effect, bold wallpaper creates a focal point, whilst plain paintwork blends into the background. Hide the fact they're cupboards altogether by fitting touch release hinges so there's no need for handles.

Everything looks better after a good clean

There are more thrilling things in life than cleaning. Some people see it as a waste of time, and it's certainly true that domestic work is never done: merely existing in a home creates mess and constant work. And there's even more of both if you have children and guests.

A thorough spring-clean and declutter are essential. Clean windows let in more light, which makes the place look bigger, whilst a good declutter will make space literally and emotionally.

Having a clean and polished background also means everything you 'layer' on top will look sharp and neat. Even an inexpensive plain white bathroom looks good when it's clean and sparkly.

To run your house efficiently (and thus happily), you need to make the daily 'processes' of looking after it as smooth and niggle-free as possible. Domestic chores are hassle enough without the process of getting organised to do them becoming a stress.

SIMPLIFY THE CLEANING PROCESS

If you have to spend ten minutes wrestling the ironing board free from the understairs cupboard, you're less likely to get it out in the first place. Not only that, it puts you in a bad frame of mind and you'll have lost ten minutes of ironing time. So keep your cleaning materials and tools accessible.

Cramming your cupboard with a million and one products makes it harder to reach the items you really want. Edit them. You need a surprisingly small number of products once you find out what works (see page 44). Storing them in a caddy keeps them all in one place and makes cleaning the house easier.

Organising the recycling, the compost and the general kitchen rubbish is part of everyday life, so work it out in such a way that suits you to avoid a build up.

KEEP CLEAN TO MAKE CLEAN

You'll never feel like you've got a tidy kitchen if your sink isn't clean and well organised. Keeping a few key essentials at the sink allows you to give it a quick once-over while you're in the kitchen making a cup of tea. Keep on top of the washing-up too. Avoid the 'it's soaking' excuse and just do it. That way it doesn't build up into a complete mission.

Don't overlook cleaning the dishwasher once in a while (especially if you don't rinse your plates before you load). Run an empty wash every few months with a dishwashing tablet and a squirt of mild bleach to blitz the insides clean.

A mouldy smell in the washing machine? It happens. To get rid of it, run a hot cycle with a little bleach and an empty drum. A natural alternative is tea tree essential oil. To prevent the mouldy smell in future leave the door open between washes. Be careful of inquisitive pets though!

Three tips for a downsized utility room

1 It's possible to put washing and drying machines on top of one another within a standard kitchen unit to make a small laundry area. If you don't have a dryer, fit shelves instead to hold powders and liquids and baskets of washing and ironing.

2 Make use of all the clips, brackets and racks you can. Use them to store tools either on the inside of cupboards, the back of a door or a wall.

3 A rack on the inside of a full-height cupboard makes the perfect home for an ironing board without losing too much valuable cupboard storage depth. Fittings for most boards and irons are available.

*Beauty and the beast. Even the most uninspiring products can be turned into beauties. Decant your shop-bought cleaning fluids into good-looking bottles (don't forget to label them or you won't know what's what). Keep function in mind and choose bottles and other containers that are fit for purpose, with a pump, pouring lip, spray, wide neck or easy-to-remove lid, as needed.

Quick clean, slow clean

A quick clean is about keeping your place tidy on the surface and relates to a sense of charm and mood: where you make things look good. The slow clean goes deeper, where you clear and clean at the same time, moving furniture, washing and wiping surfaces, vacuuming and dusting, and which gives a deep sense of satisfaction and order.

THE TEN-MINUTE DASH

You've just landed back from work and you've got friends coming for dinner, due to arrive in ten minutes...where do you start?

✳ Pull up the blinds and draw the curtains back properly. Letting in more light is instantly uplifting. If it is dark outside, you need to take the opposite approach (but then leave this step to last) – draw the curtains, dim the lights and turn on some table or floor lights to add atmosphere.

✳ Open a few windows to get a flow of fresh air into the house. You only need a few minutes of this if it's cold outside.

✳ Declutter. Clear the floor and surfaces of things that shouldn't be there. Don't worry about putting them away – put them in your 'lost and found' box so each family member knows where they will be. (See pages 36–37 for more ideas on decluttering.)

✳ Plump the cushions and straighten throws on sofas and chairs. Shine the mirror and taps in the bathroom (it makes it look like you've done the whole room).

✳ Brush or vacuum the floors. This has a huge impact.

✳ Spritz a little room spray around to freshen things up before popping the kettle on or cracking open the wine.

MAKE YOUR OWN CLEANING PRODUCTS

Eco-friendly products are kinder all round. You can make many of your own by raiding your kitchen cupboards.

MALT VINEGAR makes an excellent all-round cleaner when diluted 50/50 with water. Decant into a spray bottle for cleaning glass and mirrors, into a mop bucket for the final rinse on wooden floors, and into a washing-up bowl for other interior surfaces. Don't use it on antiques or paintwork.

WHITE VINEGAR is the traditional limescale remover. Apply to a rag or kitchen towel, wrap around your taps, leave to soak (the time will depend on how badly crusted they are – you may have to repeat the process), then wash off with soap and water.

LEMON JUICE can be used as an alternative to bleach, although some stains may need a second treatment. It also brings copper and brass back to life.

BABY OIL or OLIVE OIL are great for cleaning stainless steel but use sparingly. I always have a bottle of baby oil in my prop kitbag to keep kitchen splashbacks looking their best for photoshoots.

BAKING SODA or BICARBONATE OF SODA makes a good all-purpose cleaner or scourer when made into a paste with a little lemon juice or water. Use salt with lemon juice if you need something more abrasive (but give this a miss on stainless steel). It's also great for refreshing a pet bed when you haven't got time to, or can't, wash the cover. Sprinkle with a couple of teaspoonfuls and leave for 15 minutes or so before brushing off.

ESSENTIAL OILS such as eucalyptus, pine, lavender and tea tree are natural disinfectants. Mix with hot water and decant into a spray bottle or add directly to the mop bucket.

Utility works

Having a dedicated space for your cleaning kit, with space for a washing machine, tumble drier and drying rack, plus somewhere to do the ironing and a room to store linens would be sheer bliss.

We haven't all got that luxury though, but it is perfectly feasible to still keep things organised and feel on top of things even where space is limited. Whether your laundry 'room' really is a room or it's just a few shelves of a store cupboard – the same tips and pointers apply.

THREE TIPS FOR THE LINEN CUPBOARD

1 Keep a drawer in each room as a mini linen cupboard. Beds with integrated drawers are also extremely useful for storing bedlinen and towels.
2 Traditionally, the linen cupboard shelves were organised by room. This is probably the best method if you have purchased specific linens for particular rooms. Alternatively, linen can be organised by size so it is easy to pull out the right sheets without making a mess. Place newly laundered linens at the bottom of the pile rather than the top. This way, you don't end up using the same set over and over – you want the wear to even.
3 Making a 'bag' for the linens for each room from a pillowcase is also a good way of keeping sets of sheets together and ready for the next change. In rooms where space is at a premium, this can hang on a hook on the back of the bedroom door or at the back or side of the clothes cupboard.

THE PROJECT:

LINEN WATER

Linen water can be expensive, but it is so easy to make yourself. You only need high proof vodka, de-ionised water (you can buy this really cheaply in bulk from your local car supply shop), and lavender, lemon verbena or geranium essential oils to scent the water.

HOW TO:

✳ You'll need to sterilise the bottle you're using first with boiling water – let it dry before you start. I make mine in a glass 750ml bottle, so you'll need to scale up or down this recipe accordingly.
✳ In the cool, dry bottle, mix together 1 teaspoon of essential oil with 90ml vodka. Close the lid and shake to mix.
✳ Add the water and close the lid and shake again.
✳ Store the bottle in a cool dark corner to keep fresh.
✳ Spritz towels and linens with the linen water after washing, and on the bed each morning after making it. You can also add it to your iron when ironing.

Keeping whites white

✳ Be meticulous when it comes to sorting fabrics for the wash. Whites with whites, creams with creams. No colours should be mixed in anywhere. It makes all the difference.
✳ Dry your whites outside on the washing line whenever you can. Sunlight brightens whites naturally.
✳ Use an in-wash bleach product every six months or so, or when you need it.
✳ Treat your washing as you would your washing-up. You wouldn't wash your pans before or with your glasses, would you? Do the same with your clothes washing. The bath mat (which can get dirty) shouldn't go in with the towels.

MAKING THE MOST OF WHAT YOU'VE GOT

Most of us live in relatively small spaces in the company of too many possessions, but space is far too valuable to waste.

Assess your things and analyse your space as an interior architect would. Look at the rooms within the house. Are you using the right room for the right purpose? Then go beyond the house itself and consider the exterior spaces. Could the garage or shed be converted to accommodate your needs? A shed can be so much more than a magnet for DIY and gardening clutter.

Looking at the contents of the room, are the sofa, sideboard and table in the right places? Does the bed need moving? Resist adhering to the same layout for years on end just because that's how it's always been. Take a weekend to shift some of your big pieces around. I guarantee the results will be surprising. Similarly, keep altering your environment as your needs change, as you acquire new pieces, or simply when you get bored.

Changing the layout brings a fresh outlook, a new view on things and doesn't involve much effort at all. It is fun, free and invigorating. Trust your instinct. Sometimes the only way to get things right is by trial and error.

The way you use your rooms and arrange the furniture aren't the only things to consider. Try to look at the furniture and accessories themselves with a new eye every now and then. Could something be repurposed or moved to a different part of the house? Chests, bookcases, mirrors, wardrobes, boxes and baskets – all these can work in the places where you'd traditionally not think of using them.

Next consider renovating and reviving what you have. Paint or spray tables and wooden chairs, reupholster a chair or a stool. Most of us can no longer afford or abide the buy, buy, buy mentality. If that includes you, discover the joy of reinventing a neglected possession.

A house is constantly evolving. We can never say it's 'done' or completely 'finished'. There are always new ways of looking at it, new things to add. You might go on holiday and bring back some mementos you wish to display. Or perhaps you discover a wonderful new artwork or take a fancy to a particular item that starts you off collecting.

As a stylist, I'm constantly reinventing sets – painting a backdrop, putting up a shelf or hanging a mirror. Finding new ways to see things both at work and at home is what makes me tick. I think it's one of the most enjoyable parts of home-making.

So in order to exploit and enjoy the landscape you live in, think like a stylist or an interior architect. Use your home to tell your ever-evolving story.

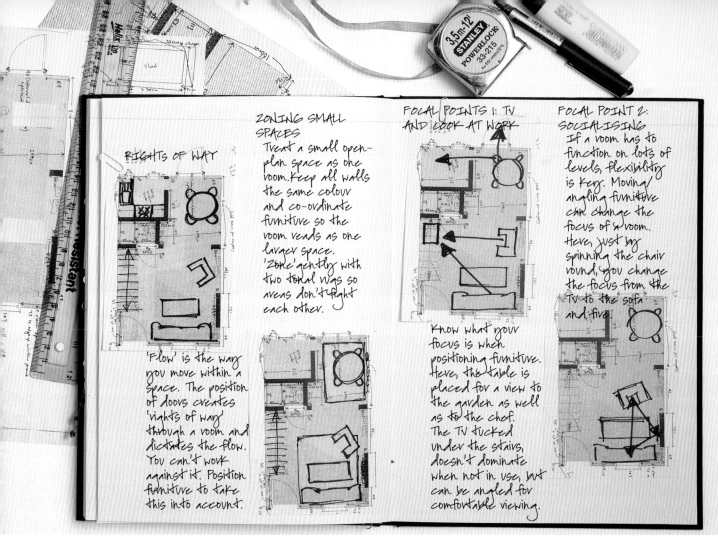

RIGHTS OF WAY

'Flow' is the way you move within a space. The position of doors creates 'rights of way' through a room and dictates the flow. You can't work against it. Position furniture to take this into account.

ZONING SMALL SPACES

Treat a small open-plan space as one room. Keep all walls the same colour and co-ordinate furniture so the room reads as one larger space. 'Zone' gently with two tonal was so areas don't fight each other.

FOCAL POINTS 1: TV AND COOK AT WORK

Know what your focus is when positioning furniture. Here, the table is placed for a view to the garden as well as to the chef. The TV tucked under the stairs, doesn't dominate when not in use, but can be angled for comfortable viewing.

FOCAL POINT 2: SOCIALISING

If a room has to function on lots of levels, flexibility is key. Moving/angling furniture can change the focus of a room. Here, just by spinning the chair round, you change the focus from the TV to the sofa and fire.

Make the most of your space

Space is far too valuable to waste, especially if you're short of it. This is true whether you're thinking about your house as a whole or about the individual rooms.

Take a long hard look at the way you use the space between the four walls you call home. Are you making the best use of the space? Don't feel you have to stick to 'traditional' room roles. A spare reception room doesn't have to be a dining room if you always eat at the kitchen table. You should also avoid the classic wastes of space – the guest room that only gets used once or twice a year, the formal dining room that you save for Christmas and birthdays, the room that's used as a dumping ground. It's fine if you've got plenty of rooms to spare, but not so fine if you're desperate for a home office, a den for the kids or perhaps a music room.

Sometimes it's not the use of the rooms that's the problem, but the layout of the furniture. It could be that it just needs a tweak to give you a layout that's both practical and feels right.

FOUR STEPS TO A LAYOUT THAT'S PRACTICAL

1 Avoid blocking the 'flow' of a space by keeping furniture away from where people need to walk. As a general rule, allow 60–75cm width as a walkway. Also allow room for long limbs to dangle off sofas and chairs, for pulling back a chair from a table so you can stand up or sit down, and for manoeuvring as you work in the kitchen (see pages 194–221).

2 Don't block access to cupboards and chests of drawers either. You need to be able to stand back from your wardrobe to see your clothes properly and pull open a drawer fully to access the items at the back.

3 Don't obstruct heat sources if you can help it. A sofa right next to a radiator is not good for the sofa and a radiator beside your head in bed is not good for you.

4 If you've got a large multi-functional space, it helps to 'zone' it into specific areas, breaking down the open-plan space into rooms within a room (see box, right).

FOUR STEPS TO A LAYOUT THAT FEELS RIGHT

1 Work out where your focus will be within the room. There could be more than one. Will you need chairs and sofas facing each other for ease of conversation or directed towards the TV?

2 Get the relationship right between the room's different elements – the angle of a pair of chairs in relation to the sofa, the coffee table in relation to the side tables. This is about giving yourself space to move around (see 1 and 2 , opposite) as well as about how you feel in that space. It should feel graceful not awkward.

3 Think about the views – to the outside through windows and doors, but also the 'look-throughs' to other rooms. A painting in one room can also be appreciated when seen from another, soft lighting filtering through from one room to another gives a warm homey feel. With these things in mind, try to position your sofa, chairs and bed in a spot where you can take in a view.

4 Sometimes, the only way to get it right is by trial and error. If the rejig involves heavy lifting, 'test' the layout first by lying on the floor where your bed might go or by sitting on a dining chair where you're thinking of putting the sofa. If they don't feel right, you'll have saved yourself a lot of hassle.

Zoning

Learning a few tricks of the trade makes all the difference between a multi-function room that works and one that's a disorganised, unfocused hotchpotch.

✳ A change in flooring works as a visual and psychological device: a different colour or textured flooring signals a change in function as well as in feel. Next time you're in a department store, note the flooring. Shoppers linger longer around the TVs and electricals because there's thick pile carpet underfoot (think rug under your coffee table at home) and they move swiftly between departments where there's sheet vinyl (think polished wood floor between coffee table and kitchen area).

✳ Different flooring also acts as a frame, helping to visually 'contain' the furniture in that area.

✳ Using the walls also helps to separate different areas. Painting or wallpapering part of the room in a different colour or pattern creates the divide, as does hanging a piece of artwork or a mirror within that zone.

✳ Use furniture to visually carve up an area. A large open bookshelf, a console table or a sofa can all be used to separate off one area from another. It's perfectly OK to have a piece of furniture with its back on show in the middle of the room. If it's looking uncomfortable, try 'anchoring' it. A pair of lamps on top of a sideboard, colourful books or objects on a shelving unit or a fur throw draped over the back of a sofa will all do the trick.

See the familiar differently

Avoid the knee-jerk reaction of chucking out the old and buying new. Look closely to assess what you already own. Can it be given a new life simply by relocating or repurposing?

Everyone can feel a little lacklustre about their home every now and then, even when there's nothing really 'wrong' with it. Things become a little samey. You can have the most fabulous things in your home yet still become a little tired of them. That's when you need to think like a stylist and get your creative juices flowing.

TRY A NEW LAYOUT

Something as simple as a switching the sofa over with a pair of chairs, say, or moving the bed to the opposite wall can give a room a new lease of life. Play around, rejigging and repositioning your furniture to see if there's a layout you'd like to try for a while. It not only brings a new energy to a room, but also changes the flow, how you move around within the space. And it can literally change your outlook, as the views you take in will be different.

RELOCATE BETWEEN ROOMS

Moving a piece of furniture from one place to another can change the way you use a room. It came as a revelation to me recently to find that a wing chair that had been cramping my lounge, when moved to what was a bit of a lost corner in the bedroom, suddenly gave me a whole new usable space. All of a sudden I had the perfect spot to paint my toenails or catch up on some reading. It was a novelty to sit in that once-annoying chair and see my bedroom from a totally different angle. It's made my bedroom into a different space and the lounge is much better for it too.

SWAP ACCESSORIES

I like change and I love coming up with new ways of looking at things. It's a pleasure for me to discover new groupings or pairings that work. I stumble across many of these successes simply by having given it a go.

Artwork, mirrors, rugs and lighting are great candidates for relocation. They can look completely different in one room to how they look in another. I'll often swap my bedside lamps with my desk lamp, or simply swap the shades on two lamp bases to revive a space.

THINK BEYOND THE USUAL

When relocating things, start with anything that isn't working hard or earning its keep in its current position, but think outside the box. A bed quilt could become a chair cover, a tablecloth or even a wallhanging. A chair doesn't always have to be a chair – it can be a bedside table or a 'plinth' for an artwork or a vase of flowers. Likewise, a bench can be part-seat, part-console table. Get creative.

Making good

DENTS IN CARPETS

Get rid of the dents left in carpets or rugs when heavy furniture is moved by spraying them with water, allowing it to soak in for an hour or so, then using a hairdryer on its hottest setting over the dents until they dry. Use a coin to fluff up the fibres.

DIRTY MARKS ON A WALL

A general residue of dust and soot can leave marks on the walls when you come to move pictures. To remove, first vacuum the area. Hold the vacuum attachment a good way away from the wall as touching the wall will spread the dust. Then use a sponge dipped in warm soapy water (washing-up liquid is fine) and, working from the outside in, dab at the stain. Rinse the sponge after each couple of dabs. Be patient; the stain should come off. But don't be tempted to rub.

PAINTWORK TOUCH-UPS

It's difficult to blend paint touch-ups in perfectly, but it's worth seeing if you can get away with it before painting the whole wall. Use a paintbrush to feather the paint, applying several thin coats rather then one thick one. When the paint is dry, give it a very light sanding with fine sandpaper to take the 'newness' off.

Renovate and revive what you've got

Making over is a great way to breathe new life into once-loved items. The possibilities are endless once you start to see the design potential in things. Chests of drawers, wardrobes, tables, an old chair with its stuffing spilling out – all can be given a facelift, either with some basic DIY skills or with the help of a professional.

Painting and spraying

It's really quite astonishing just what a difference paint can make. That old-fashioned piece of brown furniture that you wouldn't normally ever look twice at, is elevated to the perfectly chic with a couple of coats of solid colour.

What to paint: Anything that you love the shape of – the surface finish and colour won't matter. It's possible to buy a specialist primer for most surfaces, including metal and even plastic, as well as wood, so the choice is almost limitless.

The basics: Prepare the surface first, removing any old paint and varnish with wire wool, paint stripper and plenty of elbow grease. You'll need to 'key' the surface so that the new paint will adhere. Do this by sanding with fine sandpaper.

The finish: Choose from a dead flat, matt, satin or gloss paint finish according to the look you want to achieve. Bear in mind that any surface imperfections will be more apparent on a flat matt finish than on a shiny gloss finish. And take into account drying times in between coats when choosing your paint. Water-based paints dry much quicker than oil-based ones.

The application: Brush, paint pad, roller or spray – choose a method of working that you feel comfortable with and that works for the scale of the piece. I like to use mini rollers for painting the 'flat bits' of furniture and then a small paintbrush to fill in or work through any fiddly bits. If you're after a super-sleek glossy finish, use spray paint. With a little effort and lots of time it's possible to get a good-quality finish yourself, but for best results, have the job done by a professional (search online for your local car sprayer).

THE PROJECT:

A painted headboard

I snapped up this retro bamboo headboard for a song while I was shooting at a street market for this book. I loved its swirls and curves but hated the kitsch bamboo. I knew that once it had been painted white, its lovely shape would become the main focus and the bamboo would cease to be dominant. This technique works for any un-upholstered piece you might come across, whether that's a chair, a table or a headboard.

HOW TO:

✳ Prepping the surface of the piece before painting is key (see left). This will have a huge impact on the overall quality of the finish so don't rush this part.

✳ Use masking tape to mask off the edges of any areas that you aren't painting (I didn't need masking tape for the headboard as it was all painted), then apply at least two coats of primer to all surfaces. For a piece like this one, with lots of surface detail, it's quicker and neater to use spray paint. If you're painting a flat unadorned surface, apply the paint with a brush and a mini roller. I find it's better (and cheaper) to keep applying coats of primer until you can no longer see the original colour.

✳ Once dry, follow with your final paint colour. You'll need at least two coats for good coverage, possibly three, depending on the paint you're using. Sand lightly between coats with fine-grade sandpaper to give a professional, smooth even finish.

Wallpapering

Wallpaper is a great design device. Even though the days of a feature wall are over (for now anyway), there are plenty of ways to use wallpaper other than on all four walls of a room.

FAVOURITE WALLPAPERING IDEAS

✳ Wallpapering is a brilliant way to make over furniture. It works perfectly on a chest of drawers (see right) or on cabinets and bedside tables, and can be used on tabletops too. Cover papered tabletops with glass to protect against wear and tear.

✳ Use pattern to define an area of the room by, say, papering inside an alcove where a desk stands.

✳ Link two disparate pieces of furniture by papering the wall behind the two. A papered wall behind a shelf above a base unit creates the feel of a dresser.

✳ Wallpaper makes a great alternative to a traditional headboard. Keep it plain and simple within a rectangle that's the same width as the bed and as tall as one to two widths. Alternatively, go for a more ornate design with twiddly edges.

✳ Keeping wallpaper behind closed doors – on the back inside wall of a wardrobe or inside the doors of sideboard for example – allows you to bring in pattern without it overpowering a scheme.

✳ Use scraps or leftovers of wallpaper for wrapping presents.

*Use wallpaper to turn an ordinary box into something pretty. To ensure clean cuts use a sharp scalpel. Secure the paper in place with strong double-sided tape.

THE PROJECT:
A chest of drawers

Wallpapering is one of my favourite furniture overhaul tricks. It works every time, whether on a junk-shop find or on a brand new flat-packed high street bargain. You'll get a professional finish as long as you don't rush and are really careful about cutting the paper to exactly the right size.

HOW TO:

✳ Start by painting any areas of the chest that you won't be papering. If you're starting with an old chest of drawers, you'll need to prep the surface carefully (see page 57). I like to match the paintwork colour to the background of the paper, but a contrasting colour would work just as well.

✳ Next, cut the wallpaper (using a new blade in a scalpel and a steel ruler for a clean, straight edge) to fit the fronts of the drawers and the side panels of the chest. Consider carefully how to deal with the repeat of the pattern. I find it's best to have the repeat matching when the drawers are closed.

✳ Stick the paper in place slowly, one drawer front at a time, using strong PVA glue and pushing out any air bubbles with your fingers. It's easier to apply the glue to the drawer front rather than to the wallpaper.

✳ Once dry, seal with clear varnish to prevent wear and tear, and finish with decorative handles.

*The level of fiddliness involved in wallpapering a piece of furniture depends on its design. It's much easier to wallpaper flat verticals and horizontals than curves where you'll have to cut the paper and shape it around the detail.

KNOW WHEN IT'S WORTHWHILE

Professional upholstery isn't cheap, especially when it involves a complicated job like buttoning or an overhaul of the structure. So at what point do you just not bother and buy new instead? It all comes down to value, quality and price. Does the piece hold sentimental value for you? Is it a well-made antique with a solid wood frame? Compare the price of the refurb with buying a brand new piece of similar quality.

FABRIC CHOICE

The fabric has the biggest impact on the look and overall feel of the finished piece. Think about what you want to achieve. Consider colour, texture and pattern. Do you want to use just one fabric? Or mix and match?

MAKING CHANGES

If the structure of your piece needs overhauling, it offers the chance to make some changes. You might like to add buttoning or remove it, or you could change a loose seat cushion to a fixed one. But remember the golden rule – don't fight the piece of furniture. If you're unsure take the lead from the expert.

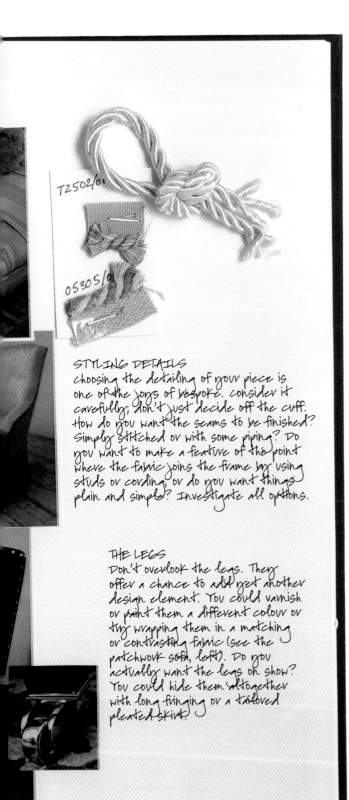

T2502/01

05305/01

STYLING DETAILS
Choosing the detailing of your piece is
one of the joys of bespoke. Consider it
carefully; don't just decide off the cuff.
How do you want the seams to be finished?
Simply stitched or with some piping? Do
you want to make a feature of the point
where the fabric joins the frame by using
studs or cording, or do you want things
plain and simple? Investigate all options.

THE LEGS
Don't overlook the legs. They
offer a chance to add yet another
design element. You could varnish
or paint them a different colour or
try wrapping them in a matching
or contrasting fabric (see the
patchwork sofa, left). Do you
actually want the legs on show?
You could hide them altogether
with long fringing or a tailored
pleated skirt.

Reupholstery

If you have the time and the inclination, it's perfectly possible to learn how to reupholster a piece yourself. Knowing that you've given new life to the piece would be a joy. Alternatively, if you aren't up for (or up to) doing it yourself, have a professional do the hard work for you. This isn't a cheap option but it's well worth the investment if the piece holds sentimental value for you or is well made. If it isn't top quality, perhaps think about getting a (much less expensive) loose cover made instead. Online companies offer this service at prices that are considerably lower than you might expect.

FOUR STEPS TO THE UPHOLSTERY OF YOUR DREAMS

1 Enlist the help of a good upholsterer and take their advice. It can be hard to visualise the finished piece and you'll be making a big investment, so you don't want to get it wrong. Choose an upholsterer whose style makes a good marriage with yours. It's important to be able to ask 'style' questions like, 'What do you think about this patterned fabric on that chair?' or, 'Will fringing look better than piping?' You need to be able to trust the answers. Go by the style of the upholsterer's shop or workroom and the kind of pieces they work on, as well as by the quality of their work.

2 Get practical. Once you've found your upholsterer, ask more practical questions too. Will it be possible to use that thick mohair and have a nice flat seam? Is this a practical, hardwearing fabric? I'm a firm believer in trusting professionals who do their job day in, day out. They know the pitfalls and how to avoid them.

3 Take photos of chairs that you like the look of as reference. That way, if you don't know all the correct terminology, you can use the photos to get your points across.

4 This is your chance to be creative and come up with something unique. Don't feel you have to upholster the entire piece in one fabric. You could select one fabric for the back section and a contrasting fabric for the rest. Remember, too, that the devil is in the detail – consider carefully buttoning, piping, skirting, pleating, fringing and edging. These all impact the final look of the piece. Adding castors? Changing the legs? The choice is truly endless. There's no reason why you can't pick and mix all your favourite features.

Wrapping and cladding

As well as painting or wallpapering the surface of a piece of furniture another of my favourite tricks is to clad or wrap them with fabric, leather or sheet metal.

WRAPPING

This technique is best for tabletops with an overhang as you can cover the top of the table, then bring the edges over and under to secure everything in place on the underside of the table. I use sheet zinc metal (search the internet for your nearest supplier), oilcloth or fabric for wrapping tables. Zinc is perfect for the kitchen or garden, a pretty yet practical oilcloth is great for a playroom, and sewing tables are a joy to use when wrapped in fabric padded underneath with felt or quilting fabric (no more lost pins). The technique is pretty much the same for all the materials (see opposite).

CLADDING IN LEATHER

Cladding with leather is surprisingly easy and professional-looking but the leather isn't cheap, so choose a small project (the top of a tray perhaps, or the inside of a box) if you're on a budget. The key to success is in the measuring and cutting. Use sharp scissors or a scalpel for clean cuts and a strong glue (carpet glue is good) applied to the leather. You can clad just the door and drawer fronts or fold the leather over the edges as I did on the bedside table, right. It all depends on the shape and style of the piece you're working with.

*To wrap a table in fabric or oilcloth, simply place the fabric (right side up) on top of the table. Use a staple gun to secure the fabric in place on the underside of the overhang, pulling the fabric as tight as you can. Secure the mid-points of the sides first, then work on the corners – just as if you were making a bed.

The little touches

The devil is in the detail. The smallest things can make all the difference to your renovated piece. Consider them just as carefully as the larger decisions about colour and finish. Knobs, pulls, legs, castors, drawer linings – all these matter and all can play their part in elevating the overall quality of the finished piece. For instance, think of the handles as being like the furniture's jewellery. You might like to spray them with a new colour or perhaps swap them for more decorative handles. Your choices are endless. Take your time.

THE PROJECT:

A zinc tabletop

This table lived in my kitchen for a while but now it's covered in zinc and lives in the garden. Zinc sheeting comes in either an untreated (shiny) or a rather unconvincing 'weathered' finish. I prefer to buy it untreated and let nature take its course. If you don't want it to develop a patina, seal it straight away.

HOW TO:

✳ Have the zinc cut to size. Allow enough excess to wrap the zinc comfortably under the table.

✳ Lay a few blankets and a layer of newspaper on the floor, then lay the zinc right side down on top. Make some guide marks on the zinc in pencil to ensure you centre the tabletop on it correctly. Apply a thick layer of ultra-strong glue to the table top, then place it upside-down on the zinc, following the marks. Place something weighty on top and wait for the glue to go off.

✳ Once the zinc is secure, begin to fold the sides up and over the edges of the tabletop. Secure in place with flat-headed nails, starting first with the midpoints of each of side, then working your way out to the corners.

✳ At the corners, make the equivalent of a hospital corner on a bed sheet. Cut away the excess zinc using a hacksaw, then file off any sharp edges before turning the table right side up.

Learn the art of display

Carefully curating the things that you've chosen to surround yourself with brings your personality home and adds your stamp. What you put together and how tells your story.

CURATE YOUR COLLECTIBLES

We all have our reasons for feeling drawn to particular items. Harness your passion for these things to pull together a collection that is unique to you.

✳ First, a word of caution about collections. Once your friends and family hear that you're a 'collector', adding an item to your collection becomes their perfect fall-back present for all occasions, so be careful how you explain your collection to them. Be very specific about what it is you're collecting. If it's 1950s white ceramics that you're interested in, say you collect 1950s white ceramics and not just any old white ceramics. If you don't do this, I absolutely guarantee that you'll be on the receiving end of lots of well-meaning presents that won't fit with your collections.

✳ Use a theme to hold a collection together and prevent it from looking like clutter. Colour, texture, mood and feel, date, style or discipline – all work as themes.

✳ Choose where to show off your collection. Perhaps you want it to sit behind glazed doors? You may need to commission a carpenter to build a bespoke unit to house it.

✳ Floating shelves (those with no visible means of support) are one of the simplest and most successful ways of housing and showing off your collections. Position books, photos, objects, vases and other curiosities in edited groups on the shelves so each group works in harmony with the next.

✳ Keep your arrangements focused and simple. Three of something off-centre on a shelf is just as effective as a straight line of several like objects. Less can sometimes be just as impactful as masses.

✳ Change your displays around whenever you feel like it. This always refreshes the energy in the room and also makes you see your possessions anew.

ARRANGING EVERYDAY TREASURES

Once you start to view your belongings through a stylist's eye, you'll see potential beauty in displays of even the most mundane objects, not just your artwork or collections. Artfully arranging your bits and bobs will give you endless chances to create visual moments, or vignettes, that will make you smile.

SEVEN TIPS FOR CREATING VIGNETTES

1 There's no need to theme your vignette. Creating a vignette is more about combining things just because you like them. You'll get as much pleasure from the playing, editing and rotating as you will from the finished display. A vignette can be as simple as adding a postcard and a vase of flowers to a pile of books beside your bed, or it can be as elaborate as rearranging all kinds of things you've collected over the years on top of a large sideboard.

2 Think about the display from front to back and in 3D. How do things cross one another and overlap from the front and from above? And what about from side to side? How is the overall shape of the display working? Use varying heights to add interest.

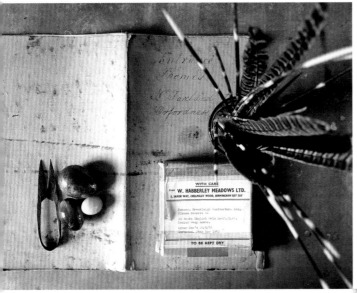

Create a 'plinth' from a pile of books or use a small block of painted wood to stand smaller objects.

3 To make your vignette look considered and curated rather than just a jumble, contain it within a 'frame'. This could be a horizontal 'frame' such as a mirror, a tile, a tray, a large hardback book, or even an unfolded map. Or use a vertical 'frame' such as a painting, or mirror to sit your treasures in front of.

4 Add something unexpected – a bow around the neck of an animal figurine or a kitsch something or other amongst your serious art. Show off your sense of humour and personality.

5 Use the walls– they aren't just for artwork and books. Commission a carpenter to build a series of shelves or boxes specifically designed for your treasures. Or track down old drawer tidies (see above, left), that can be painted and hung on the wall to display all the little things.

6 Make your everyday treasures more impressive than they really are by using the same display devices as you would for 'formal' art. Set a simple vignette of small treasures in a glazed display box or on top of a plinth to make it into something special. I also like to use glass cloches to show off small-scale displays.

7 See beauty in everything. Once you start to use these display tricks you'll be able to turn almost anything into a vignette. Beautiful ribbons and buttons accompanied by a single flower will suddenly take on a whole new life.

Creative Chaos

Put together what I call a 'dream wall' to create a very personal decorative focus. It's a chance to indulge your creativity purely for creativity's sake. Make it a constantly evolving display of memorabilia, visuals you love, things that inspire you and things that you aspire to. Position it according to how much creative chaos you can live with. My threshold is low, so I confine my dream wall to my shed, aka, mini studio (see page 234).

*To tame your creative chaos ever so slightly, use pictures of the same size and don't overlap them. Also, give it boundaries within a clearly defined area. Alternatively, don't have it on show at all but confine it to the inside of a cupboard door to give you a buzz when you open it.

Display tricks for kids

Give your children the chance to display their treasures in their own personal space. It's just as important for children as it is for adults. With an adult's guiding hand, children can curate their possessions in a way that they find pleasing. It will help make them feel responsible for their belongings and will encourage them to keep their things tidy too. It will also help them understand and respect the value of other objects in the home.

*Providing a place for children to show off their favourite things can be as simple as a shelf for teddies, books and other toys, or as elaborate as a whole wall of wooden boxes such as this one. The interior of each box has been lined with patterned wallpaper and given a lick of paint, and the boxes hung in a random pattern.

Hanging your art

Putting up your paintings, framed photos and prints is one of the finishing touches that makes a home truly your own. Take time and care to display them properly.

IN AN ORDERLY FASHION

Arranging your artwork in neat rows and columns is the classic way of hanging art. It's very clean and graphic, and allows the art to be the focus. It's time to get the spirit level, tape measure and pencil out; artwork hung this way needs to be bang on.

USING AN 'ANCHOR' AND AN 'ANCHOR LINE'

When deciding where to hang your art, imagine there's a grid running over each wall and consider where any furniture that sits against the wall falls within that grid. Using the imaginary grid as your guide, take the centre line of a key piece, for instance the chest of drawers (see below), the pair of beds (see right) or the pair of chairs (see below right), and follow the line upwards. This is your 'anchor line'. Position your artwork centrally on this anchor line, as if the anchor line were cutting down the middle of the artwork.

The same rules apply if you're hanging one piece of artwork or masses; you simply build outwards from the anchor line. You can use more than one anchor line if you like but imagine if you could pull the anchor lines up to lift the furniture from the floor, would your artwork display be balanced in relation to the furniture? If not, the anchor lines are in the wrong place.

When deciding on the height at which to hang your artwork, you need some horizontal lines to aid you. Look to any architectural features in the room for these horizontal reference lines or 'floats'. You might have the top or bottom of a window frame, a horizontal line in a room's panelling, the line of a picture rail, the top of a mantelpiece or the line of the shelves in a built-in bookcase. Imagine the 'floats' sit on top of the water line and imagine them bobbing up and down as the water line rises and falls. You will be hanging your artwork 'on the water line'. There are no strict rules to follow to get the height right; just be aware of your room's reference points and go with what feels right.

THE FREEFORM CLUSTER

This is one of the easiest and most relaxed ways to display your art. You don't even need to worry about everything being in line or even straight (you can put the spirit level away now).

You could throw caution to the wind and just start hanging, but I prefer to have a dry run first before committing to the wall with the hammer. My dry run consists of laying out the pictures on the floor and playing with them, adjusting the layout until I'm happy.

I find it easiest to start with a key piece – either the biggest or the one with the most vibrant colour. This will be where your gaze rests first. Once that's in position, work outwards to position the rest.

When you think you've cracked it, take a photo. Once you start moving the artworks to hang them on the wall, the shape of your layout will disappear and it's surprisingly difficult to piece it all back together quite so perfectly second time round.

To make your cluster look carefully curated rather than simply flung on the wall, line up just a few of the artworks. The line doesn't have to be absolutely exact, just exact enough to look considered.

A freeform cluster works particularly well when it goes wall-to-wall – one whole wall in a playroom, say, given over to posters and paintings, with the other walls bare. The calm of the three clear walls balances the intense wall of art.

Containing the display within two imaginary uprights or 'anchoring' it to a piece of furniture (see pages 76–77) – above a table or sofa for example – will help a cluster look thought-through.

Landings and stairwells are also perfect places for clusters of artwork. It's always tricky to work out how to hang multiples in a space where there are lots of levels going on, but you can hang a cluster here pretty much any way you choose without having to worry about what happens when you reach the stairs (see right).

LEANING

You don't always have to hang an artwork; you could just lean it against the wall instead (see top right). This gives a much less formal look and also allows you to move pieces around or swap one piece for another as and when you want. What is more, you won't have to

worry about having holes in the wall.

Leaning is most successful when you use a real mix of sizes and frame styles. Layering is key too, with the smaller artworks at the front and the bigger ones towards the back.

Displaying works by leaning rather than hanging allows you to add unframed items to the mix. Postcards, paintings on boards, even invitations can all form part of your artwork display and such a display can also be the starting point for a vignette (see page 66).

If the surface you're standing your frames on is quite slippery and they keep wanting to slide down, a tiny amount of Blu-Tack discreetly placed on the bottom of the frame should do the trick.

GO HIGH, GO LOW

Art does not always have to be hung at eye level; it can be fun to experiment with other options. A series of small pictures can look stunning when hung from the top of the wall to the bottom in one continuous vertical line. Equally, you might hang a large picture at eye level, with a series of smaller pictures below.

DISPLAY SHELVES

A series of floating shelves is a practical way to showcase your artwork. Their pared-down, minimal looks help to make the paintings or sculptures the focus. Painting the shelves the same colour as the wall will heighten this effect. Standard floating shelves are widely available to buy, but it's still hard to find shallow shelves with a lip on the front that are specifically made for leaning pictures. So, you'll need to make your own (see box, right).

THE PROJECT:

A leaning gallery

Create a gallery on shelves for your artwork, collections and family photos to fit the space you have. Galleries work best when they run the whole width of the wall.

HOW TO:

✳ Measure the area for the shelves and decide how many shelves you need, based on the height of the things you want to display. For each shelf, buy smooth sawn timber cut to the correct length as follows: one length of 94mm x 18mm (A) and two lengths of 44.5mm x 21mm (B).

✳ To form the lip on the front of the shelf, screw the widest side of one of the short pieces of wood to the narrowest side of the longer piece.

✳ To form the upstand at the back of the shelf, screw the narrowest side of the second short piece to the widest side of the longer piece.

✳ For a professional finish, countersink all screws using a countersinking bit on your drill. Fill the holes and sand before painting to match the walls.

✳ To hang, drill holes at regular intervals along the upstand, then attach to the wall using plugs and screws.

USE ART FOR COLOUR
Art adds colour to an otherwise neutral scheme. It won't overpower the room like a wall of bold colour can, and it adds contrast and texture too.

LET ART BE A BACKDROP
Don't be too precious about covering parts of your art. A large painting hung low can form a backdrop, with lights, furniture and other accessories in front.

USE AN ANCHOR
'Anchoring' your art in relation to key furniture works for freeform clusters as well as for rows of art (see page 15).

*

tiny
positioned
off-centre at
eye level

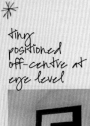

Supersized to create a focal point

THINK INSTALLATION
The style of frame you choose is sometimes almost as important as the artwork itself.

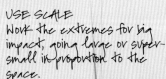

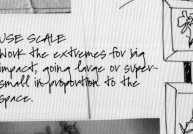

USE SCALE
Work the extremes for big impact, going large or super-small in proportion to the space.

SHOW THE WORKINGS
It can be attractive to see the artwork's hanging device but for this to work, choose the best-looking fittings.

Children's artwork

It's hard to know what to do with the huge volume of works that budding artists amass. As an auntie to sixteen, I've had my fair share of paintings and cards over the years, but I see the amount that my nieces and nephews bring home to their parents.

So how to deal with it all? I think you need a three-pronged attack. First, go for a tight edit. Choose your or your child's favourite and put that on display. Second, containment. Give the work a designated area in the house – on a mantelpiece, in the hallway, in the kitchen – and stick to it. And third, rotate – regularly swap an old piece of work for a new one.

THREE WAYS TO DISPLAY

1 Create an artwork 'washing line', either using a tensile wire kit with metal clips (widely available and sold as a curtain-hanging system) or simply with string or garden wire and clothes pegs. Depending on how much space you want to dedicate to it, attach one or more lines in rows under each other down the wall.

2 If you are short on wall space, hang a colourful ribbon down the middle of the back of a door with a drawing pin top and bottom. Then use pins to attach drawings to the ribbon. It works best for smaller works. This is also a good way to extend your 'washing line' display – simply tie the ribbons to the line.

3 Cluster paintings and drawings together en masse. Either go freeform and let the display flow out at the edges, or contain it within an area and keep overlapping.

*Make a thing out of displaying a child's artwork and your child will feel honoured that his or her work has been given space in the home. The way you style it up will make the display look considered and a proper part of your interior scheme.

Other ways to bring children's artistic talents into the home

✳ Ask children to write the name cards for your next sit-down family party. Younger children can stick to just the name with a decorative motif; older children could try and draw a portrait of each guest.

✳ Wrap your presents in plain paper (brown parcel paper or wallpaper lining paper) then let children loose with felt tip pens, coloured pencils and crayons.

✳ The formality of working on a canvas rather than on paper elevates what would be just a nursery painting into a real artwork. Art shops sell ready-stretched canvases quite inexpensively. Display the masterpiece in the same way you would any other kind of artwork.

Make books part of the scheme

If you like reading and like holding on to your books, you'll eventually get to a point where you need to consider what to do with them all. Embrace them as part of your décor and treat them as decorative objects in their own right.

BUILT-IN STORAGE
Made-to-measure shelving maximises the space you have for books. It's not cheap but is well worth the investment. Although dedicating an entire room to a library will remain just a dream for many, it is possible to create the feel of a library on a much smaller scale by lining one wall, or even just a small section of a wall, with shelves.

ARTFUL ARRANGEMENTS
Arranging books according to colour can look stunning but it isn't the most efficient way to organise a large number of books – it works best if you have a small collection and a great visual memory. Alternatively, mix in 'objects' among your books – to create a balance between display and storage.

Tips on made to measure
✳ Consider architectural features such as doors and windows. Use them to your advantage and incorporate them into your design, fixing shelves around or above them.
✳ Utilise the unused. Spaces above head height in landings, hallways and corridors are often overlooked and are perfect for bookshelves.
✳ Painting the shelves 'out' to match the colour of the walls will make them feel less intrusive.
✳ Measure the books you need to store – are they art books or paperbacks? – and build your shelves accordingly.

MAKE THEM EARN THEIR KEEP
A pile of books, positioned against a wall or side-by-side creates a 'block' that is sturdy and heavy enough to use as a side table beside a sofa or bed (see left). Pile them up to the required height.

Books, especially larger hardback ones, can also come in handy as styling tools to use all over the house when putting displays together. A pile of books will add height to tabletop arrangements and provides the perfect 'plinth' for a vase, a candle or a cup of tea on a coaster. It can also be an object to sit on.

BE A MORE CONSIDERED SHOPPER

For some, shopping is pure pleasure and a brilliant pastime, while for others it can be a dreaded necessity. For all of us however, shopping takes time and effort and some considerable thought. Whatever your predilection, one of my rules is that you should never make a purchase based on panic, lack of time or because the item is cheap. It doesn't matter how little or how much something costs, if you feel it is right, it will be right. Hence my belief that you should only ever buy those things that you want, need and love. Spend your money wisely and never consume for the sake of it.

Shopping is a skill but considered, careful shopping is an art that everyone can learn. I have learnt to be a professional shopper through my work as a magazine editor. It has trained my eye to discern the difference between well made and poorly made, between beautifully conceived and designed, and shoddily thought through. Shopping professionally has also taught me how to weigh up whether or not a piece will fit a space and a certain style of living.

If I had to summarise the things that will make you a better shopper, it would be the following five points:

1 Compile a list of your needs and wants and prioritise them. I give some guidelines to getting this right on page 86. This will bring structure and focus to your shopping expeditions.

2 Do your research. This is the most critical part of the shopping process. Make things easier for yourself by doing much of the legwork online before going out to see the items you have identified as possible purchases. Buying – especially big-ticket items – without seeing the thing for real, is dangerous and not for the faint-hearted!

3 Aim to find one or two things at a time. Buying in bulk isn't the path to successful shopping. Add to your home or collection slowly and with care.

4 Look beyond the price ticket. Sometimes it pays to spend that little bit extra (see page 88), but sometimes a bargain will fit the bill too (see page 91). Just remember, though, a bargain is only a bargain if firstly, it is something you want or need, and secondly, if it works with your particular space.

5 Shop around. By comparing lots of items closely, you'll gain greater confidence in your ability to recognise quality and value and in making the right call. Doing the research on the internet (see point 2 above) is always a good backup as well. It aids the learning process and you never know where it will take you…

Getting your shopping priorities right

Take a good, long, perhaps even hard, look at your home and the day-to-day needs of the household. Think of your rhythm and your routine, and what niggles you the most on an everyday basis.

Inadequate plumbing, bursting drawers, kicked-off shoes, tumbles of books, coats hung one atop the other obstructing the entrance, piles of laundry (clean and dirty) with no dedicated place to be stowed away – these are the sort of things we experience all too commonly. It's fascinating what we are willing to live with, what becomes 'normal'. Look at your home as if you were seeing it for the first time, identify key problem areas then buy yourself out of them. In my experience, these are the areas where spending money will result in a happier home. You won't regret it.

THE BONES OF THE BUILDING
Treat any problems that are part of the 'bones of the building' as your number one priority. Get to the bottom of the damp patch on the wall beneath the window; discover why the wallpaper in the lounge is peeling; replace or reglaze that draughty window before the next harsh winter. It will save you money in the long run as you'll nip a potential disaster in the bud, but it also makes basic good common sense to ensure that the roof over your head and the walls that protect you from the outside world are secure.

MEETING YOUR BASIC NEEDS
Shelter, warmth, hot running water, and peace and quiet are the basics we expect from our homes. A roof that lets in water, radiators that don't heat a room properly, inadequate plumbing that leaves the last one up with a cold shower, or a bed that is robbing you of a decent night's sleep all need dealing with. Get them fixed as soon as you can afford to do so.

SOLVING DESIGN PROBLEMS

You can solve design problems by buying the right piece of furniture, be that a large cupboard to serve as a larder or the right sofa configuration for your open-plan kitchen/living space. What you are looking for, apart from shape, proportion and colour, is a piece that will make a difference to you, both emotionally and practically. Does that sofa fit the space and give you enough seats? Does that cupboard look great and store all the food you want it to store?

MAKING THE EVERYDAY RUN SMOOTHLY

It's all about process. If you've sorted out the right bin system for your recycling, there won't be annoying piles of rinsed plastic and waste paper building up beside the bin. If you've organised how best to deal with your laundry and found a permanent home for the iron and ironing board, you'll never again fret about getting it out of sight when friends come over for dinner. Give thought to the most efficient way to organise and carry out the everyday tasks. It will make them easier to manage, but it will also make them less noticeable and intrusive.

SOLVING YOUR STORAGE PROBLEMS

Lack of space is many people's problem and lack of storage only exacerbates this, making a space seem smaller than it really is. Do spend on storage solutions for things like winter jackets and boots, summer clothes, household admin and the children's school and sports bags. What you need is storage that's easy to use. It makes being organised and keeping things in the right places automatic.

Making an investment

Nine times out of ten you can spot when something was really expensive. A little something will give it away, be that the quality of material, a clever design detail or the perfect colourway.

Deciding when to invest and when you can get away with spending less is something that you must work out to suit your needs, budget, personal preferences and taste.

WORTH THE EXPENSE

It's up to you, but in my opinion there are three cut-and-dried reasons why it's worth paying over the odds for something:

1 If a piece of furniture was conceived by a well-respected designer and/or high-end manufacturer or design house. You're buying into the prestige. Its resale value should hold as many things become collectors' pieces, so such items are normally a good investment.

2 If top-quality materials were used to make the piece or if a specialist manufacturing technique was used that, for example, took two years to perfect, it's common sense that it's going to be expensive. Research and expertise quite rightly cost money.

3 If it has been painstakingly and lovingly made by hand and the process was a lengthy one, it shouldn't be cheap. You're paying for labour and artistry. That's not to say that all things handmade are expensive; many offer exceptional value for money (see page 111).

Love is in the air

Buying something you love is one of the great pleasures in life. It doesn't necessarily have to be an expensive purchase but it should be the best of its kind for you. You know if it's right as it will make you smile and make your heart sing. A purchase of this kind can be symbolic – of age, achievement or a personal success – and so will always stand for more than its physical self. It might be a vintage table lamp as a treat to yourself after a pay rise, or a piece of artwork for you and your partner to mark an anniversary. When you've got it home, it makes you feel good to gaze upon it, but there's also pleasure to be had in the simple act of just putting together a list of the things you love. My current would-love-to-buy wish list includes a Fornasetti black-and-white cabinet, a pair of Antelope chairs by Ernest Race for my garden, a large-scale floral painting by Parisian artist Claire Basler and a brand new black lacquer upright piano. These are all items that are way way down in terms of priority on my shopping list, but... I hope their moment will come.

*It sometimes takes just one amazing piece mixed in among lots of carefully selected cheaper high street buys to make a room sing. It's the equivalent of partnering an expensive pair of shoes with a cheap dress.

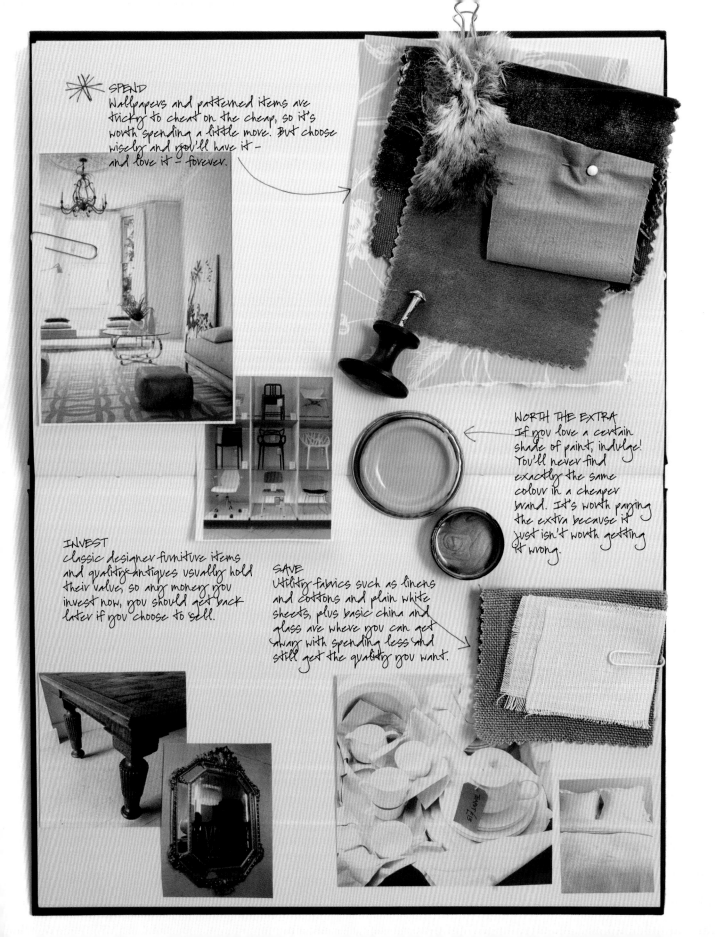

SPEND
Wallpapers and patterned items are tricky to cheat on the cheap, so it's worth spending a little more. But choose wisely and you'll have it – and love it – forever.

WORTH THE EXTRA
If you love a certain shade of paint, indulge! You'll never find exactly the same colour in a cheaper brand. It's worth paying the extra because it just isn't worth getting it wrong.

INVEST
classic designer furniture items and quality antiques usually hold their value, so any money you invest now, you should get back later if you choose to sell.

SAVE
Utility fabrics such as linens and cottons and plain white sheets, plus basic china and glass are where you can get away with spending less and still get the quality you want.

Shopping for the long haul

Most people recognise that it is sensible, preferable and, in the long term, economical, to spend money on their big furniture items. But the financial, emotional and style commitment involved in buying for the long haul can provoke such a case of nerves in people that they resort to the mistake of opting for a cheaper, short-term buy.

The key to longevity is to buy the best quality you can afford, in a style you'll hopefully want to live with in years to come. Knowing what you'll love in ten years' time can be hard to predict, but buying into your signature style will help future-proof your purchases. A table or chandelier that fits your own unique sense of style rather than a particular trend put together by someone else is more likely to work for you over the years as your look evolves. If you can, investigate the next price band up from where you normally buy – the extra investment may be worth it. It's also wise to stick to classics. Anything that's 'of-the-moment' won't stay that way for long. When replacing expensive items such as sofas, bespoke curtains or armchairs, opt for a plain or a classic pattern fabric (a stripe, a check or a damask) as nothing dates faster than pattern. Quality antiques are usually well made; if an eighteenth-century chest of drawers has stood the test of time so far, it'll probably manage another 50 years in your home. Or commission an antique of the future and invest in the craftsmanship and artistry of today (see opposite).

The definitive guide to commissioning a one-off

Commissioning a one-off piece for your home is a valuable and often extraordinary experience. You are buying pure bespoke, something made-to-measure for you and your home. That it could be an antique of the future gives it added value, but the real reason for wanting bespoke is that the result is unique.

✳ Decide on the piece you want to commission then consider your budget. Your craftsperson may be able to help you on the budgeting side of things by making minor adjustments to the design to help shave a bit off the cost, or perhaps by taking payment in instalments to spread the cost.

✳ Find your craftsperson or designer-maker. Search online crafts and art websites, visit local galleries and attend open studio events and college shows. And don't worry; you'll know when you've found the right person as you'll feel a connection with their style, work and personality.

✳ Meet to discuss the design, budget and timeline. Ask to see examples of their previous work. Don't overlook delivery costs and VAT. Discuss what would happen if things go wrong. Talk about what both parties' expectations are.

✳ It's standard practice to put down a deposit or part-payment before work begins and some designers expect an interim payment. These payments could be anything from 5% to 50%. You may be able to view the work in progress.

*The piece you commission doesn't have to be a 'precious' artwork in the traditional sense (an oil painting or a sculpture). There's joy to be found in everyday 'functional' artwork such as bespoke cabinetry and tableware.

Do sweat the small stuff

If you drink from a particular cup every day and you sleep for eight hours each night; if your glance out of the window takes in a certain garden pot; and if the knocker on your door gets rapped by every guest, it feels right and proper to buy the cup, the mattress, the bedlinen, the pot and the door knocker thoughtfully and with quality in mind.

Buying quality items that are part of your everyday life will make a big difference to how you feel every day. The experience of drinking wine with a daily meal is improved when it's served in a delicate glass. A simple salad tastes better eaten with cutlery that have a bit of weight to them. Your morning tea or coffee will be worth getting up five minutes earlier for if you serve it in a nice mug. Sleep will come easier and restless nights will be a little less hard to bear if you've invested in a decent set of bedlinen and the right mattress for your back. Going to bed and having a meal or a hot drink will all become rituals to be savoured.

THE MEANING OF VALUE

What does value mean to you? The Oxford English Dictionary definition is: 'the regard that something is held to deserve, the importance, worth, or usefulness of something'.

Value is in no way the same as cheap; value is the balance of quality and price. It's a simple equation: price + quality = value. Everyone's equation will be different, according to their priorities. An expensive item can be perceived as good value if it's beautifully crafted from quality materials that will last for years. Buying a low-quality 'bargain' that needs to be replaced time after time won't seem like such a bargain for long. Your ethos should be to buy once, and buy well.

There's nothing to say, though, that cheap is bad. Especially when you're on a tight budget, buying something cheap can allow you to splurge on a more expensive item. The high street, DIY stores and discount outlets all offer good-value items at low prices. Train yourself to think about the lifespan of an item, its quality of manufacture and materials, and then decide if it's right for you.

---

*The small things can alter the quality of the chores, the rituals, the experiences we have every day in our homes – and this can have a knock-on effect on our happiness. Choose carefully the things that matter most to you – take pleasure in the seemingly mundane.

Sales shopping without tears

There isn't such a sense of seasonality to interiors items as there seems to be with fashion – nor such a quick turnover in our homes. Most of us don't have the urge, the need (or the cash) to replace and update homes items at the start of each season. Unless you're made of money, it would be madness.

✳ Use the sales to re-stock basics and buy long-lusted-after expensive classics. If you have enough time to be a bit strategic and do some forward planning, you can buy things as and when they come up in the sales. That way you won't miss out on anything other than the higher price tag.

✳ To get the best deals you need to be organised. Think through what you'd like in your home before you actually need it. That way you can pick things up when the price is right (such as buying red flowers just after St Valentine's Day instead of in the run-up to it).

✳ Keep a long-term shopping list somewhere so that you can refer to it easily. As you think of them, add to the list of things that need replacing (towels), that you'd like to upgrade (pots and pans) or that you need to buy new (those fabulous cushions, that to-die-for set of espresso cups). If you like having people over to stay, don't rush out in the days leading up to Christmas to buy their towels and bedlinen. Instead plan ahead of time and buy in the summer or mid-season sales before the guests arrive. I can't remember the last time I paid full price for fluffy white towels, cotton sheets, pillows or plain crystal glasses.

Bedding essentials

Your choice of pillows and duvet is an all-important part of giving yourself a good night's sleep in real comfort, so make a point of finding the right type of pillow and duvet, be that in down, silk or synthetic.

DUVETS AND PILLOWS can be filled with either a natural (duck feather and down, goose down or silk) or a synthetic filling. Duck feather and down are heavier (and generally cheaper) than goose down. Think about your personal preference. I like to feel secure in bed and enjoy the weight of duck feather and down and I struggle to sleep under just a sheet when on holiday somewhere tropical.

Depending on your washing machine's capacity, it is possible to wash a feather or down duvet at home, but it needs to be dried thoroughly. This is problematic with a domestic tumble dryer. Firstly, the dryer will probably be too small for the duvet (unless it's a single or a cot duvet) and secondly, drying can take far longer than you think. Even when the duvet's touch-dry, it's probably still damp in the centre. It's best to have it professionally cleaned – though I do wash my duck-down duvet in the washing machine when I know the sun will be shining and the day very warm so I can hang it out to dry.

SILK is a good alternative as a duvet filling for those with allergies to feathers and down. To care for your silk-filled duvet, air it out in the sun once a year. The ultraviolet rays in sunlight kill off germs. If the duvet needs to be cleaned, it must be done professionally (this can be done every other year if there have been no spills or accidents).

SYNTHETIC fillings for duvets and pillows are a good option for those with allergies. They are also practical if you need to wash or have your duvet cleaned often.

MATTRESS TOPPERS will help to protect your mattress as well as adding an extra layer of comfort. They range from quite flat (adding minimal extra padding) to almost duvet-like wool-filled quilted designs. Choose according to your needs. You don't have to add a purpose-made topper – you could simply use a cotton or fleece blanket underneath your sheet. Just make sure it's large enough to be tucked in properly.

THINGS TO THINK ABOUT WHEN SHOPPING FOR BEDDING

✳ **Duvets** Any allergies? How warm/cool do you like to be? Do you prefer a heavy- or light-weight duvet? How easy is it going to be to keep it clean?

✳ **Pillows** Any allergies? How much support do you like? How many pillows do you prefer? Do you need large square pillows that will prop you up comfortably for reading in bed?

✳ **Mattress Toppers** How much extra cushioning do you want? How much protection do you need?

Tog ratings

The higher the tog number, the warmer the duvet – it's all about how well the duvet traps the warm air. Duvets with natural fillings are better at trapping the warm air than synthetic ones, so they require less filling. That means a duvet with a natural filling will be lighter than a synthetic one. It's possible to buy an 'all-seasons' duvet. This consists of two separate duvets – one lightweight (for summer) and one medium weight (for autumn and spring) – that can be buttoned together to make up a heavyweight one (for winter).

What's the deal with sheets and thread counts ?

While thread count is important because it indicates the quality of the weave, when buying bedlinen, don't get too caught up with thinking the higher the thread count the better. Sheets made from cotton with a very high thread count (the count can go up to 1000) can be quite fragile, so aren't actually that practical. Opt for a minimum of 180 if you can, though 220 is better, and 300 and 400 are better still. Try to buy from a reputable manufacturer; the way the cotton has been treated and finished really will affect your overall comfort.

Towels

Choosing towels is as personal as buying bedlinen. The higher the grams per square metre (gsm), the heavier and more absorbent the towel will be. A good-quality towel should neither shrink nor shed too much in the wash.

TERRY TOWELS are conventional, fluffy towels. The heavier the weight, the better the wear and absorbency.

WAFFLE TOWELS are woven cotton towels that are lightweight and absorbent. They are practical in summer as they dry out much quicker than terry towels.

HAMMAM TOWELS are either textured (generally made from tufted or looped hemp or from a linen–cotton mix), or finely woven cotton, usually with fringing at the ends. The latter are great to take on holidays as they pack down to virtually nothing.

LINEN TOWELS are beautifully indulgent, extremely absorbent and available in a range of woven patterns and designs embellished with monograms, embroidery or stitching.

Caring for your towels

✳ It's always a good idea to wash a new towel before you use it as it will have been sitting around in the shop, but it will also help to remove any excess lint which will shed all over your bathroom.

✳ Generally, all good-quality towels become more absorbent the more you wash them, however, if you are a white-towel-person, never ever wash your towels with any other coloured items. White only stays white if washed with white-only items.

✳ Soften up a 'crispy' towel that has been dried on a radiator or out in scorching sun by whizzing it in a tumble dryer for three or four minutes with a damp cloth spritzed with a little lavender water. Better still, don't leave towels on radiators or in the sun to the point where they're 'cooked'. I refuse point blank to use fabric conditioner in a towel wash as I believe this reduces their absorbency and changes the 'feel' of the towel.

✳ If you catch the towel and a loop is pulled out, it's ok to snip it off. Your towel won't unravel.

CHOOSING THE COLOUR

White towels always look good and have an air of luxury. Black, muted greys and taupes are much more practical and just as chic. If you want to layer in extra colour, choose carefully, as the moment you add burgundy or yellow towels to the mix, you risk the effect becoming somewhat student-like. Turquoise and sea/sky blues are always nice to add, especially in the summer months. I prefer to leave bold, bright patterns and colours for the beach.

SIZE MATTERS

Face cloths or flannels are handy to have in large quantities as they need washing very frequently. I use pure white to go with my white towels, but I have a few extra in dark colours so that I don't ruin the white ones when I'm taking off make-up.

Hand towels are an opportunity to add a bit of your style to the bathroom, as they come in many patterns and colours. When guests are in the house, I put out a mix of vintage embroidered towels and classic flat weave linen towels. Your friends will appreciate both the effort you have made and the experience of using them.

Bath towels should be large enough to cover your body from chest to mid-calf. They are generally labelled 'bath sheet' or 'jumbo bath sheet'. They feel luxurious because of their size, but they can be heavy to use, take up a lot of storage space and are bulky in the washing machine. I find that towels simply labelled 'bath towel' are perfect for wrapping round your head to dry your hair or for children under the age of ten. Too small a towel is a misery, but equally, too large can be cumbersome.

China

Most of us use the general term 'china' to talk about ceramic tableware regardless of whether it's made from porcelain, earthenware or stoneware. So, what is the difference between the 'china' types? It lies in the various clays used, the minerals that are added and the temperature at which the clays are fired.

EARTHENWARE is fired at a low temperature so can be quite fragile and can chip easily. It's also porous, so needs to be glazed. You can also find 'vitreous hotel-ware'. This is fired at a higher temperature and is usually a little thicker so that it's more robust.

STONEWARE is fired at a higher temperature, which makes it stronger than earthenware.

PORCELAIN is made from a white clay and is pure white and translucent. It is commonly referred to as 'fine china'.

BONE CHINA – the clue's in the name. A key ingredient is ash from animal bones. This china is pure white and very translucent. It's also much stronger than it looks as it's fired at a high temperature.

BUYING SECONDS

Many high-end manufactures sell off as hugely discounted 'seconds' – pieces that have failed their stringent quality controls. This is a great way to buy into a quality product at cheaper prices. Armed with a little expertise, it's possible to cherry-pick pieces that have only very minor, almost indistinguishable faults. Stick to plain china seconds, as patterns tend to highlight any flaws – but remember, seconds are seconds for a reason. Things to watch for are:

✳ Overall shape and size: Avoid any obvious wibble wobbles. Study the pieces from all angles, individually and side-by-side if you're buying a set. Watch for the thickness of each item too – are the cups all the same thickness at the lip? Plates the same at the edges? Some flaws may only be noticeable once they are stacked. Decide if that bothers you, bearing in mind that it probably won't be noticed at the table. A fractional difference here or there won't be spotted.

✳ Unevenness in the glaze: Flecks, drips and wiped-off glaze are a no-no. Tilting the item so that the light catches the glaze will help reveal any irregularities. Make sure the colouring is consistent across a set you're piecing together.

✳ Above all, don't rush. Take your time and sift through the stock to pick out the best pieces that work together in a set for you.

Cutlery

Cutlery is an everyday essential. Getting it wrong can seriously reduce your chances of enjoying a meal while getting it right can elevate your experience at the table.

SOLID SILVER is a soft metal and will scratch – over time it will develop a lovely patina. Each piece should be hallmarked.

SILVER PLATE is made when silver coating is applied to cutlery made from a mixture of copper, zinc and nickel. The quality of the plating depends on the thickness it's applied in (measured by weight in microns). The minimum is 20 microns.

STAINLESS STEEL stains less readily than other metals. The higher the nickel content, the better the quality.

THINGS TO THINK ABOUT WHEN SHOPPING FOR CUTLERY
✳ The feel: formal or informal? It's obvious that solid silver in a traditional design is meant for fine dining, but there's no reason why you can't use your solid silver every day to add a touch of class to your life.
✳ The finish: silver, silver plate or stainless steel? It all comes down to price. Solid silver isn't cheap. I buy up solid silver pieces in Old English-style when I see them at the right price. Most modern designs only come in stainless steel, so the choice has already been made for you.
✳ The design: modern or traditional? This relates to the feel you're after (see above), but bear in mind if you want multiple sets of cutlery; good-value bistro-style plastic-handled cutlery works well for garden parties.
✳ How many pieces? A place setting for each person comprises seven pieces – two knives and two forks (for main and starter), a soup spoon, a dessertspoon and a teaspoon. Many designs are sold in sets without the starter knives and forks. If this is the case, you may want to buy two sets so that you don't have to wash in between the courses of a dinner party.
✳ The weight: heavy or light? The cutlery should feel nicely balanced in your hands.

Caring for your cutlery
✳ The best way to clean all cutlery is by hand, although most new cutlery is dishwasher-safe.
✳ In the dishwasher, don't mix silver with other types of cutlery such as silver plate or stainless steel. The metals react together and discolour.
✳ Use a gentle detergent, preferably liquid not powder.
✳ Don't put vintage pieces in the dishwasher; they weren't made to be washed in a dishwasher.
✳ Don't put cutlery made from two materials in the dishwasher; the joint between the two will be ruined.
✳ Don't soak cutlery for long. It will end up spotting.
✳ Regular use is the best way to keep silver from tarnishing.
✳ Store silver cutlery that isn't used regularly in an anti-tarnish canteen, cloth roll or airtight container.
✳ Solid silver and silver plate need polishing every now and then. For a quick, home-made cutlery polish, mix bicarbonate of soda with enough water to make a toothpaste-like consistency.

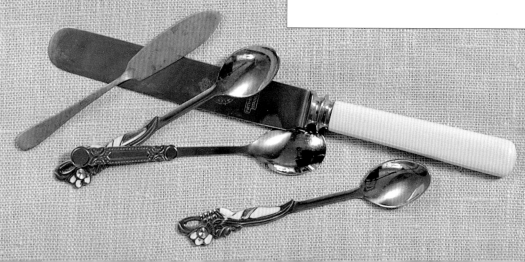

Glassware

When it comes to style, the choice is endless. Patterned or plain? Coloured or clear? Stemmed or goblet? And that's even before you've decided which type of glasses you need in your set.

LEAD CRYSTAL is made when lead oxide is added to molten glass. The lead oxide enhances the sparkle of a glass. Most 'formal' glass is made from lead crystal.

PRESSED OR MOULDED GLASS generally offers good value. It's made in a mould, often with a textured pattern and with colour. Most designs tend to be in thicker glass, so it's normally quite robust – one for the garden table.

ETCHED AND ENGRAVED GLASS is where plain glasses have been given a surface decoration after the glass has been formed. Etched patterns are created by applying an acidic or abrasive substance to the glass, while engraved designs are made using tools that cut into the surface of the glass.

CUT GLASS normally feels heavy for its size as thicker glass is generally needed for the pattern to be cut out. It looks beautiful on a candlelit table as it reflects light.

THINGS TO THINK ABOUT WHEN SHOPPING FOR GLASS
✴ Consider what weight you prefer in your hand (and on your lips). A fine glass will have a thin rim, while a more robust design will feel chunkier and heavier to drink from.
✴ Also consider how accident-prone you are.

Delicate, long-stemmed glasses may not be for you if your overexcitable dog will be rocking the table.
✴ It makes sense to buy everyday glasses in a slightly thicker glass so that they stand up to the wear and tear (and the dishwasher). A basic 'everyday' kit would include: tumblers (short and squat, for juice and neat spirits), hi balls (tall and straight-edged, for water, cordials, beers and spirits with mixers) and bistro-style wine glasses (slightly thicker glass with a short stem, for wine).
✴ For some, a wine glass that's designed specifically for each wine is a must; for others the basic 'larger bowl for red, smaller for white' will suffice. Tailor your collection to your needs. If you're a big grappa fan or are massively into Belgian beer, treating yourself to the right glasses may bring you even more pleasure.
✴ Glasses can be used for all sorts of things. Tumblers can double as candle votives or vases, and can be used to serve individual portions of desserts such as trifle or fool. Try cocktail glasses and champagne coupes for these mini desserts too. Shot glasses can be commandeered for use at parties to serve tiny portions of soup or mousse – or use them as mini-vases with a tiny flowerhead in each.

Become a hunter-gatherer shopper

It's possible to head to a large high street store and find pretty much everything you need, but that 'decorating-by-numbers' way of buying, as I call it, is rather predictable and means that you'll get a home that looks just like lots of others on your road, in your town and in towns like yours.

Branching out and sourcing things from different places will make your home much more individual, interesting and original. Bring things back from your holidays, trawl the antiques fairs and markets, hunt down treasures that will tell a story. Pieces that are unusual and hard to find won't be what everyone else has. What's more, this type of shopping helps develop your sense of style.

HOLIDAY SHOPPING
Shopping when I'm off travelling is one of my favourite pastimes, an absolute must wherever I go. It could mean a leisurely trawl of the flea market stalls lining the street on the way to get breakfast in Paris, a strategic stop at a specialist glass store in the centre of Istanbul with the taxi metre running, or a walk round a reclamation yard down the end of a country lane on the way back from a weekend away. It's not just about the treasures you might track down, but the experience itself – the sights, the smells, the things you learn and the laughs you have along the way. It's about bringing home a story and filling your home with items that hold a history that's personal to you.

What you decide to buy will depend on your signature style and where you're travelling to, on how much money you want to spend and on what you need.

SOME OF THE THINGS I'VE BOUGHT AND LOVE LIVING WITH:
✳ Silver hand-cut flowers from Mumbai's silver market – still in my box of treasures. Simply lovely just to look at.
✳ Cotton hammam towels from the souk in Istanbul – great for holidays as they dry so quickly and take up no room in a suitcase.
✳ Metres of silk exquisitely embroidered with Lucknow embroidery. I use one of the lengths I have as a bed throw, and the other as a (a very posh) tablecloth.
✳ A hand-carved double-sized daybed for my garden, bought in Bali

and shipped back in a container that a friend was sending home. It truly makes my garden what it is.

＊ A galvanised steel coal shovel, the perfect size and shape. Not the haul you'd expect from the south of France!

LATERAL THINKING FOR FOREIGN SHOPPING

When you're on holiday, food markets, hardware shops, even local supermarkets can be prime hunting grounds too. There may be a local cooking utensil or some innocuous household item that catches your eye, or a unique set of storage jars, a piece of crockery or a cake tin in a shape that you've never seen before. Bringing something home that's everyday in its country of origin but is extraordinary where you live feels like a special discovery. Look also to the local rituals. The national dish? The local tipple? You'll probably be able to track down all the paraphernalia involved in serving it while you're scouring the local shops. Think tea glasses in Marrakesh, coffee grinders in Turkey – the list is endless.

THE ONE THAT GOT AWAY...

Retail regret is a terrible thing. You've probably got one already – the one thing that haunts you, that you wish you'd bought when you had the chance. For me, it's those silver-edged engraved Turkish tea tumblers from Istanbul. I wish I'd bought a job lot instead of just the six. I've learnt my lesson. If something really grabs you...grab it back and take it home with you.

Tips for shopping abroad

＊ Try to avoid the tourist rat-runs and the hotel foyer shops.
＊ Do your research before you go. Find out what the country, area or region you're going to is famous for. Search the internet for forums where travellers share their experiences and you'll get the inside track.
＊ Think about enlisting the help of a guide when you go shopping. There's nothing like local knowledge. Give in to the fact that he or she will probably be earning a percentage. That's just how it works in some parts of the world.
＊ Really think about how the piece will fit in back home and don't get too carrwied away. You're after the feel of a well-travelled home, not a theme-park version of your last destination. Design details, embellishments and colourways that look fine in their local environment and are part of the piece's charm can lose their appeal once they're in the relative simplicity of your own surroundings.
＊ Pay a fair price (for you and the local).
＊ Trade with respect and a smile. You're bringing home a story, a memory and an item to treasure.

Showcasing a well-travelled home

The secret to making your holiday purchases work once you get them home is not to overdo it. Don't go all out for 'a theme' – just bring one or two key items per room to mix in with your existing scheme.

Unless you actually want your living room to look like a copy-cat version of a Riad in the medina of Marrakesh, or your bedroom to look like a Maharajah's palace, there's no need to add any other Moroccan or Indian influences to the room other than the leather pouffes you bought in the souk or the embroidered wallhanging you picked up at the market. No fretwork, no polished plaster walls, no mosaics. No carved four-poster or printed ceiling canopies. It's the contrast and balance in a scheme that make a room interesting to look at and be in. The feel and mood, colour and texture that each item brings is what creates this balance – and it's easy to throw things off-balance.

*Items picked up on your travels are normally very different to what you'd have access to on your home turf. Use them to provide contrast in your scheme. The beauty and quality of an ornate wooden cabinet (see left) stands out even more when set against a white, minimal scheme. Likewise, the rough, rustic quality of the chairs (see right) are highlighted when placed at a sleek white painted table beneath silk lampshades.

*It's easy to feel overwhelmed by a jumble of antiques. Take things slowly. Let your eyes adjust. Step back and get a sense of the larger items first (the sofas, chairs and mirrors). Then step closer to eye up the accessories before you go in for a good rummage.

Something old...

The wonderful thing about designing and appointing a home is that everything simply cannot be new. Something old, reclaimed, reupholstered or simply renewed will add richness, personality and often an organic edge to a scheme. The richest source of this material is undoubtedly markets, fairs and boot sales.

TIPS FOR HUNTING OUT THE OLD STUFF

✳ Wear sensible shoes and clothes that you can be nimble in. You may have to jump into the back of a van or climb through masses of grubby bits and pieces to find your gem. Also, don't flash your cash; it's a day to dress down rather than up.

✳ If you're new to this kind of shopping or don't feel confident, treat your first trip as a dry run. It will take some of the pressure off and allow you to watch and learn.

✳ Get there early – the best stuff is usually sold very early in the day. Often between dealers. I've even heard of buyers pretending to be sellers and paying for pitches just so they can get into the ground early to swipe the best items.

✳ Carry cash: nearly all stallholders work on a cash-only basis. Carry plenty of change for car boot sales, as well as for the tea and bacon-buttie van (these are de rigueur at most venues).

✳ Take a torch if you're going early in the winter and the fair is held outdoors. All the pros bring one. Head torches are especially good.

✳ Bring a tape measure – and the vital statistics of the slot you want to fill – so you can make sure items will fit.

✳ Think about how you're going to get things home (measure the boot of your car). Have a back-up plan in case you find something you love and need a bigger vehicle.

✳ Don't have your ideas about what you're looking for set in stone or you'll drive yourself round the bend trying to find exactly what's pictured in your head. It's much better to have a vague idea of what you need and what the maximum or minimum sizes are that are going to work for you.

✳ Learn to understand when you have to have something and trust your instinct. If you delay, the piece will probably be gone by the time you make it back to the stall. But you need to be able to differentiate between a 'must have' because you love it and a 'must have' because you're overly excited and shopping on adrenalin.

✳ Have a good old rummage and dig deep. Rummaging's allowed, but be nice and ask for permission before moving any large items or jumping into the backs of vans.

✳ Know what you're buying. It's not uncommon now for repro items to be mixed in with antiques and vintage at fairs as well as at shops or reclamation yards.

✳ Learn how to haggle politely. I've found that by being friendly and polite you get the best price.

The hunter-gatherer's haul

Your haul will be particular to your needs and tastes and will be the result of the luck of the draw on the day. This is what I've managed to pick up over the years and have found works really well once I get it home – or have seen and lusted after, again and again, while out 'hunting and gathering'.

ARCHITECTURAL PIECES
❋ Old beams or joists – have these sawn by your local timber merchant and you could end up with wonderful wide floorboards.
❋ Fully restored radiators fitted with modern, but old-fashioned-looking valves.
❋ Doors and door furniture such as beautifully-pitted pewter knobs and gorgeous heavy door knockers.
❋ Generously-proportioned baths and sinks in perfect condition.
❋ Cast-iron window frames to use in your garden, either as they are or fitted with mirror.

FURNITURE
❋ Cheap-as-chips darkly varnished furniture to sand down and repaint (see page 57).
❋ Solid, well-built sofas and chairs that you love the shape of. It won't be cheap to have them reupholstered, but it will be worth your while if they're quality pieces.
❋ Old oak doors are always worth looking at carefully. They often come in odd sizes, which means they cannot easily be reused as doors but can become excellent table tops.

TABLETOP ITEMS
❋ Mismatched cups and saucers to build up a non-matching set (see page 98). The more colours and patterns, the merrier. Use them for tea, as vases or to store bits and bobs.
❋ Trays: silver, pewter, toile, big and small. All useful for serving food or for displaying and storing your collections.
❋ Serving ware: build up a collection of platters, oversized plates, silver-plated serving spoons, ladles and forks. One old-fashioned, overly ornate piece used in a table set together with contemporary plates can look stunning.
❋ Glasses: all kinds. I try and buy in sets or, at the least, a pair, but you could make a thing out of them not matching at all. Unmatched glasses work best with 'party' glasses used to serve guests standing to drink cocktails or champagne. Set out an eye-catching array on your party table to make an impact.
❋ Cutlery: mix and match silver and silver plate. Look for cute little serving pieces that will pretty up a basic setting. Think ornate jam spoons, coffee spoons with decorative handles, a mother-of-pearl-handled butter knife – all these are good.

What not to buy
❋ Think carefully before taking on a piece that needs restoration. Do you know how much it might cost to restore? Don't just rush in, eyes focused on the bargain ticket price, thinking it'll be all right. Take into account the cost of re-gilding, re-upholstery, French polishing...
❋ If the idea of a 'project' appeals to you, be honest with yourself and know your time and skill limits. Are you really going to learn how to reupholster a buttoned Chesterfield? It's the equivalent of buying a designer dress at a knock-down price and saying, 'I'll slim into it'. You also need to think where you'll store the piece while you get around to completing it.
❋ Make sure you always bring your vital stats with you when you shop. Don't guess at measurements – it's surprising just how 'out' you can be. If you're not sure something will fit and it's important that is does, walk away.
❋ There's a fine line between 'charmingly aged' and plain old tat. Learn where that lies for you. Think about how the piece will look in the balance of your scheme.

Buying antique chic on the cheap

Buying on eBay is a great way to buy vintage pieces that bring a bit of history to your home, even if it's not your history. Not all of us are lucky enough to inherit the family silver.

✳ Do your research to find out how much the item is worth.

✳ Decide on your limit. Obviously, you don't want to pay over the odds, but would you be upset if you lost out for a few pounds? Once you've set your limit, stick to it.

✳ If it's possible for you to be online in the final five minutes or so before the bid ends, place your highest bid at the last minute – that way no one else has a chance to outbid you.

SOFT FURNISHINGS AND FABRICS

✳ Old curtains: don't think of them as curtains, see them as fabric. Cut them down into throws or cushion covers or use them as upholstery fabric. Even if some of the fabric has deteriorated, there will probably be sections that are still usable.

✳ Cushions: look beyond the limpness. This is easily solved with a new cushion pad.

✳ Bedlinen: heavy vintage linen and cotton sheets make great tablecloths and are much cheaper than buying new. I buy even the less interesting ones, without monograms or decorative detailing, with a view to dyeing them. They look fantastic once they're a shade of indigo or grey.

✳ Rugs can be amazingly cheap secondhand. Some designs, such as flat weave kilim rugs, can actually look better with a little colour fading and wear. Remember to bring your measurements with you when you're hunting and gathering.

ODDITIES

✱ Old books: be brave and rip off the covers. Brutal, I know, but the naked books look great piled high and used as display plinths.

✱ Odd crystal knobs and knockers or odd chandelier droplets: I group them together in bowls to make table-top displays. Absolutely anything that catches your eye, makes you smile and makes your heart race.

ENLISTING THE HELP OF A PROFESSIONAL

If you're short on time, enlist a professional shopper to look for a particular item. The purchase won't be as cheap as if you'd found it yourself, but you won't have spent on petrol or parking, nor used your own time. The item will still be cheaper than if you'd bought it from a shop. Many antiques shops offer this service and may be willing to do a deal as it's much safer for them to buy a piece knowing they've got a customer to sell it on to. Alternatively, if there's a stallholder whose stock you love, ask them to find something for you.

*Search through boxes of china, glassware and cutlery, and through bin bags of linens and fabrics. Often among the tat there will be a gem lurking that makes it worth buying the whole box or bag for.

GETTING THE FEEL JUST RIGHT

The elements that conspire together to create the feel and the atmosphere of a home are elusive. We all strive for that intangible sense of balance and completeness. A home is not merely a collection of furniture, or a study in taupe. It is not a perfect replica echo from a magazine spread. It is more than paint charts, swatches, and the shallow preoccupation with beauty over reality. Yet neither is a home just the sum of our functions. It has to be more to us than the dirty pots and pans, the toilet brushes, the laundry piles, the ignored leaflets on the doormat. So what marries these two aspects, what softens the lines between the form and the function of the home? They are unifying but hard-to-touch, and we can explore them, calling them the 'non-visuals'; the many aspects of homemaking that you can utilise to create a home that not only appeals to the senses and reflects the season, but one that absolutely, utterly feels like home, your home.

The seasons are a fine and natural inspiration. They influence us; you feel differently in warmer weather than in colder. Translate this to how you dress your home. In winter, our instinct is to hunker down, retreat and shut out the rest of the world. In summer, we fling the doors and windows open and invite the outdoors in. Being in touch with the world outside is a way of informing the look and feel of our home. Change the accessories you have to suit the season – it could be something as simple as swapping heavyweight fur throws and chunky wool knits for cotton and mohair versions instead.

As the seasons shift, the light changes, and should prompt you to consider your lighting within the home. Lighting can illuminate or depress a room, directly affecting it and so impacting on how you feel within the space. If you do nothing else getting your lighting right at the very least will make a space feel warm, welcoming and finished.

Fragrance, too, alters the mood of a room, and change how you feel. Change the fragrances in your home to suit the mood and season, just as you would your perfume. In spring and summer it feels right to use sprays – they are light and fresh in application – as well as perfume (light florals, greens and citrus). In autumn and winter, I light candles with smokey, woody aromas, and incense and oil burners with essential oils like Neroli and frankincense.

One magical element that will always, always elevate atmosphere and add easy sensuality is the addition of flowers. Flowers for me are one of the most joyful parts of life. They make a room feel cared for. Not extravagant armloads of roses, or costly elaborate arrangements – it doesn't have to be remotely formal. Place a single rose in a glass tumbler by your bed, a stem of blossom, cut from the garden in the hallway. A bowl of narcissi marks the beginning of spring, an abundance of annual flowers celebrate the highs of summer. Anything that'll bring you a smile.

*Use small changes to make your home feel more appropriate to the weather. Appeal to your senses – fragrance, accessories such as cushions and throws, flowers and lighting are your tools.

Staying in touch with the seasons

The way we use our homes and the activities that take place within them change with each season. There's also a change of mood and a shifting of inspiration as the scene outside our doors and windows alters.

Our outlook changes too. Autumn and winter are more inward-looking and introspective. The curtains are drawn and windows and doors are shut, keeping the cold out and the warmth in. Outings are organised and planned, strategic. Layers of clothing are hauled on and off. There are strict rules in place to keep the elements at bay; doors closed, boots off, coat hung.

Summer and spring are much more free, and the way we live, freer. Doors and windows are flung open; each blast of fresh air is welcome; bare feet go in and out of the house and garden. Sounds and smells drift in from outdoors. There is the hum of a mower cutting the grass, the sound of a sprinkler hitting foliage from a distance, the smell of a neighbour's barbecue.

Embrace each season. Adapt your home to the changes in temperature and light. Go with your instinct. Do what feels right for that time of year.

Spring

Spring. The promise of longer, warmer days, of possibilities and of hope. I see spring as an opportunity for an official opening-up of the house for the coming months. The house sings of being clean and fresh and of lightening up.

OUTSIDE AND IN SPRING CLEAN

Of course, it's the usual time for a spring clean, a to-the-rafters sortout and declutter, followed by a thorough scrub-down. Everything looks and feels so much better when it's clean. Include the outdoors in your annual spritzing routine – sheds, summerhouses and garages all benefit from a yearly clean-out too. Care for outdoor furniture now too, re-oiling wooden pieces, wiping down other surfaces, washing outdoor cushions and de-rusting the barbecue. It means you'll be ready and organised for the season well ahead of time and you'll get the most out of any good weather as soon as it arrives.

HOME RHYTHMS

I love the idea of reinstating house-keeping rituals, like having a 'wash day'. It brings a certain rhythm to the home and the routine of doing something at a particular time means you won't forget. Each spring I wash my duvets, pillows and throws all in one go. That way I don't have to keep track of what needs cleaning.

SPRING PAINTWORK

Now's the time to refresh any paintwork that's still looking grubby after the spring clean. A word of caution, though. Once you start you may not be able to stop as your newly painted walls will show up any less-than-perfect ones.

FURNITURE REJIG

Spring is also the ideal opportunity to play with the positioning your furniture since you'll be moving it to vacuum or brush and mop anyway. A quick rejig of a few things – moving a chair here, moving a chest of drawers there – can totally reinvent a space.

COLOURS OF THE SEASON

Nature never ever gets it wrong. Look at the perfect colour palettes that surround you everywhere. There's the hundreds of punchy acidic greens of flush new growth, twenty different blues in the sky each day – then there's the masses of clashing brights of the spring vegetables and flowers. Let the combinations inspire you at home.

Summer

Summer spells freedom, barefeet and being outside. I all but decamp to the garden, eating, lounging and entertaining outdoors whenever possible, blurring the lines between indoors and outdoors.

THE LIGHT FANTASTIC

Let in as much light as possible. If you have heavy curtains, buy a pair of tie-backs to keep the curtains well away from the window. If you have blinds, pull them right up.

FRESH AIR

If you've got an outside space – use it (see below). If you haven't, bring more fresh air into your home by flinging open as many windows as you can and allowing the air to circulate.

LIGHTEN UP

I like a hot bath before bed but it just gets too hot in summer if I put on my heavy towelling robe after my bath. Instead I switch to a cotton waffle one. The same goes for my towels. Linen or cotton flat weave towels have the advantage of drying quickly – a bonus in summer when your towel warmer may not be on (see page 96 for more on buying towels).

SWAP OVER ACCESSORIES

Lighten up on your throws and cushions. Swap fur cushion covers for cotton ones, a heavy woollen blanket for a light mohair throw. It's easy to swap cushion covers if you always stick with the same cushion sizes. That way you only have to store the covers from season to season. Some people swear by swapping a thick-pile rug for a flat weave rug in summer. The key here is to have sufficient storage space to accommodate the out-of-season rug.

OUTSIDE EATING

See al fresco dining as something for every day, not just when you're entertaining. Make use of the good weather whenever you can – even if it's just a cup of tea enjoyed in the garden before work.

GARDEN FURNITURE

Don't be too precious about what you can and can't use outside. If you haven't got outdoor dining furniture, bring out the kitchen table and chairs for a meal; it won't do any harm if it's brought back in the same day. It's become a bit of a cliché to think of the garden as another 'room', but it really can be. Furniture and accessories matter here just as much as they do indoors, as do finishing touches such as flowers, linens, pretty tableware and candles.

COLOURS OF THE SEASON

Let the flower borders provide inspiration. Notice the subtle changes that occur in one flower from bud to bloom to fallen petals.

Autumn

Autumn brings both a sense of renewal and that back-to-work/school feeling. Gradually day-to-day life revolves more on being indoors. Use this precious time to enjoy family-focused activities centred around the home – bake bread and cakes or spend an afternoon making jam.

TIME FOR NEW SKILLS
This is the perfect time to discover a new craft, re-learn a forgotten one, teach your skills to a loved one and let them teach theirs to you. All those nights in front of the TV or beside the fire can be put to good use. Knit, paint, sew, crochet – whatever takes your fancy.

INDOOR PROJECTS
Tackle projects indoors that you put off during the summer months when it was just too gorgeous outdoors to be indoors, and see to any outside chores before the harsh weather sets in.

HAVE A THROW HANDY
Drape a folded throw over the back of an armchair or the end of a sofa so that it's close if you want to curl up and get cosy.

SCENTS OF THE SEASON
I like to change the way I scent my home according to the season. In autumn, I like to light candles with smokey and woody scents.

COLOURS OF THE SEASON
In autumn, a perfect colour palette plays out on the forest floor and in the canopy of the trees. Take inspiration from the multitude of yellows, greens, oranges and reds. Watch the play of shadow and light as it changes its effects on the colours through the day.

Winter

Winter's pace is slower. Go with it, enjoy it.
Use it as a chance to create a different kind of
comfort that appeals to all the senses.

WINTER BEDDING

Swap over from the lightweight, low tog duvet for a heavier version.
For extra warmth, if you use large square pillows on your bed, switch
the cotton cases for knitted covers. They tend to be a standard size,
so are easy to find. You could go the whole hog and switch to flannel
bedding; it can be chic, and no, it's not just for kids.

COSY TOES

Take the edge off the cold first thing by laying a runner or sheepskin
beside the bed if your bedroom floor is uncarpeted.

A WARM TOUCH

Drape a softening throw, quilt or blanket over a metal or wooden
bedstead or headboard in winter. The metal will feel cold to the
touch, which isn't pleasant to lean against in winter, so the throw
will counteract this.

WINTRY LIGHT

Embrace the low winter light levels by turning the dimmer switches
down and lighting a fire. Winter's a good time to play around with
lighting. Move task lights around; you may need them in areas of the
room in winter that are different from those in summer, depending
on how your activities change with the seasons.

CHRISTMAS PLANNING

Use the time between early winter and Christmas to get ahead.
Start thinking through what needs to be done and plan it in such a
way as to spread the burden both financially and chore-wise. Being
organised is the best way to keep the
stress out of the Christmas period.

FRESH AIR – YES, REALLY!

You probably won't feel like it, but
keep opening windows and doors
occasionally to let in some fresh air. It
will have an energizing effect.

COLOURS OF THE SEASON

This is my favourite colour palette of
all the seasons and one I find the most
usable in interiors – it's the perfect
inspiration for a neutral palette:
hundreds of shades of off-whites are
created with a covering of morning
frost, the perfect combination of
silvers and blues can be spotted in a
frozen river, beautiful delicate shades
of pinks and grey in a single flower,
almost pearlised with a dusting of ice.

Lighting

Lighting is one of the single most important factors in your home, it affects not only how a space looks, but how you feel within it. Lighting allows you to alter the mood and atmosphere of a room at the flick of a switch or the strike of a match to light a candle.

Harsh lighting is the biggest instant killer of atmosphere. Strip lights, undimmable single-source ceiling lights, fluorescent lights... none of these are conducive to putting people at ease. In an ideal world, we'd all have separate lighting circuits controllable within an instant of entering a room or within an arm's reach of our bed.

IMPROVE YOUR LIGHTING WITHOUT RE-WIRING THE HOUSE
But to achieve all this, you'd have to tear open the walls of your home to access the electrics and then make good afterwards. Instead, here's what you can do without having to get an electrician in and spending a fortune.

✳ Make the most of the daylight. Pull heavy curtains right back and fit tie-backs if necessary. If privacy is an issue, install a sheer blind or curtain panel; light will filter through, but you won't be overlooked. And make sure your windows are cleaned regularly; you'd be surprised how much light dirt and grime can steal from a room.

✳ Fit dimmers. Don't skimp; cheap dimmers have a tendency to buzz (it's to do with the quality of the transformer inside the dimmer). Seek advice from an expert so that you match the rating of the transformer to your circuit requirements. Some pendant lights have a built-in transformer in the ceiling rose. Check at the point of purchase that the type of light you are buying is dimmable or that your dimmer switch is compatible. It's now possible to fit a dimmer to your bathroom light, even if it's on a pull cord inside the room.

✳ Avoid using a single light source. The most common mistake is to use a single pendant in the middle of the room. Layer your lighting by adding table and floor lamps. Ideally these are on a separate circuit, controlled from a doorway, so there's no fumbling around when they need switching off and on. If that's not possible, fit an in-line switch (an on-and-off switch wired into the cable) so that they're easy to control.

✳ Choose a statement piece. Think of your lighting as another layer of decoration in your room. An amazing chandelier or floor lamp will have just as much impact as wallpaper or a piece of art and will totally change the feel of the room. Make sure it's fitted with a dimmer – you want it to be a decorative piece rather than the main light source. Remember: layer, layer, layer.

FUNCTION v FORM?

Ornate fittings are a great way to bring in decoration to a scheme - whatever your style. Make sure it's not your only source of light in the room so that you can light it according to what looks and feels best rather than practicality. Treat decorative lighting in the same way you would art or jewellery - to add the finishing touch to a scheme. It can look just as good unlit as it does lit.

THE SHADE MATTERS TOO

The material, the colour and the finish of a shade makes a difference to the mood of the light it gives off. The colour of the shade and its lining will be transmitted. Unlined shades allow the bulb to be seen through it, whilst a thick fabric will diffuse it and send the light up or down depending on the shape of the shades.

POSITIONING OF PENDANTS?

Make sure there is enough room to comfortably walk underneath an ornate fitting - at least 30cm clearance - anything less doesn't look right.

THE BULB MATTERS

Choose the right one from a safety and a style point of view. Follow the designer's recommendation.

Fairy lights aren't just for Christmas

Remember how warm and inviting it felt? Re-create that feel with trails of fairy lights. Positioning is everything – it should look considered, not plonked. Place the lights where they will interact with other items in the room, such as above a piece of furniture or framing a set of shelves. It needs to feel like a permanent fixture rather than just something left over from Christmas. Tame untidy cables by using phone cable clips (from DIY stores).

＊Play with scale. Go large or small where it's not expected – an oversized pendant in a small room becomes a design feature, as do multiples of small pendants clustered en masse. Work in the extremes for greatest impact.

＊You don't always have to have pendant fittings hanging high – have a little fun with their position. Try hanging a lamp low, either side of the bed, or as a centrepiece above a coffee table for example. You'll need to have at least 30cm free space underneath the fitting to use a bedside table easily, and a minimum of at least 60cm above the coffee table for it to work practically.

Tips for choosing the right bulb

1 Follow the bulb guidelines that come with light fittings. Never exceed the maximum wattage as you may risk shorting the fitting or the circuit in your home or even cause a fire risk.

2 The shape of a bulb does matter as does the finish. There is usually a choice between reflective (silver tipped and good for metal lamps), satin or clear bulbs.

3 Artworks look better with a clean, bright white light as opposed to more yellow tungsten light. Ask at your electrical outlet for advice and help.

4 There are many new low energy, halogen bulbs that are dimmable, so always check at your local electrical supplies store to see what is available and suitable for your light fittings.

*Make your own lamp by placing a string of fairy lights in a plain glass vessel (a wine vat, vase or any large bottle). It's simple, but beautiful when lit.

Candles

Everyone looks and feels better by candlelight.
Here are the candles I use the most in my home,
for every day and for something a little bit special.

TEALIGHTS AND NIGHTLIGHTS

The handiest type of all – cheap as chips and easy to dress up with a pretty decorative candle holder. They're especially effective when used en masse, in numbers as big as you can bear to light, and you get double the twinkle if you position them in pretty holders in front of mirrors. I also use them outside in the garden in jam jars strung from trees, and nestled into borders and beds. There's also one in the oil burner beside my desk and three in matching cut-glass holders that move from the coffee table in the living room to the bathroom as and when needed. Nightlights – a little bigger than tealights – last longer, roughly 6–8 hours instead of 3–4 hours, so use these for parties. They are great forming a row either side of the garden path to the house and/or lining the windowsills at the back of the house.

CHURCH OR PILLAR CANDLES

These are long-lasting and so are great value. Available in various sizes, colours and fragrances. To help the candle burn more efficiently, carefully push the outer edges of the candle towards the wick as the wax melts.

CONTAINER CANDLES

Normally seen in the form of scented candles in glass jars, these come in various sizes and qualities. Some are large and have a number of wicks. It's worth noting that these multi-wick candles don't necessarily burn quicker than those with a single wick, but the additional wicks help the candle to burn more evenly. I use container candles in storm lanterns for outside dining as they give off much more light than nightlights or tealights.

DINNER CANDLES

Used for candelabras and candlesticks, these give off a good amount of light. A five-branch candelabra should cast enough light for a candlelit dinner for four, giving just the right amount of atmosphere and without people having to squint to see what's on their plate. These candles come in countless sizes, colours and finishes, but I like to keep things simple and buy the pure beeswax ones. They have an exquisite amber colour and subtle honeyed fragrance. Stunning.

TWO WAX REMOVAL TIPS

1 Wax on the tablecloth: it's easily done; a nudge of the table as you rise from your seat, overenthusiastic blowing out or that drip, drip, drip from the candelabra towards the end of the evening.

To remove, wait for the wax to cool properly. Peel off the chunky bits first, then place a piece of brown paper on top of the wax and use a hot iron to melt it off. The wax will transfer to the paper.
Keep moving the brown paper around so you cover the wax with a clean area of the paper until the wax disappears.

2 Wax that's stuck in the candle holder: wax shrinks when it's cold. Pop the candle holder in the freezer for a couple of hours so the wax should come out cleanly (use a table knife to prise it out). I also use the following technique: float the candle holders in a sink full of cold water for five or ten minutes then the wax should come out easily using a knife. Clean away any residue with warm water and a sponge or cloth.

A few things to know about burning candles

✳ Keep the wick short. Trim to about 5mm each time you use the candle. A long wick burns with a larger flame and gives off more soot.

✳ Limit burn time. Follow the instructions that come with the candle as burn times vary according to size, shape, added fragrance and what the candle's made from.

✳ Position the candle carefully. Keep it away from draughts, which make the flame flicker. When this happens, the wax will melt unevenly and will be wasted.

✳ When not in use, keep candles away from heat sources – these include warm sunlight – or they'll go soft and start to droop. Store dinner candles flat so they don't warp.

✳ Put candles in the fridge for a couple of hours to extend their burn time. The chilling makes them burn more slowly.

✳ If the wick disappears deep inside a pillar candle, you have two options: either insert a tea light (it will be out of sight so nobody should notice) or cut the candle down. Use a knife to score around the edge of the candle and slowly work your way towards the centre until you've taken the top 'slice' off the candle. Trim the wick if necessary. Keep the scraps to make your own candles (see page 134).

Styling tricks for lighting outside

It doesn't take much to turn your garden into a magical space come twilight. A few candles to light the table, a row of votives to line a path and outdoor fairy lights scattered through the trees will make all the difference.

pretty punched patterns. I've lined pathways for guests to follow through meadows and woodlands at parties and weddings and they never fail to charm.

TORCHES

Torches on stout poles can be bought cheaply from DIY stores. A pair flanking a garden path or even numbers lining a walkway through the lawn look fantastic.

STURDY LANTERNS

Storm lanterns and rustic fisherman lanterns will stand up to the wind and are the perfect way to light the outdoor table after dark when nightlights just don't do the job. Far better to have a line of three storm lanterns down the middle of the table than a jumble of nightlights and no one able to see what they're eating.

CONTEMPORARY LIGHTING

If you're going to use your garden as an outdoor room in the true sense of word, you'll have to give serious consideration to the lighting in order to get the most use out of it after dark. You can now buy outdoor table lamps, floor lamps, pendants and chandeliers that enable you to treat the outdoor space exactly as you would an inside room.

BRAZIERS

A brazier can be magical; there's something really mesmerising about a real fire.

TURN OFF THE LIGHT!

While we're on the subject of creating magic outside, never ever install a security light that you can't switch on and off. A floodlit garden each time anyone moves isn't conducive to the mood.

FAIRY LIGHTS

Add magic to your garden for summer parties with fairy lights carefully strung through the trees. Weave them through the branches in a random pattern. Opt for strings with small bulbs that give off a warm white glow rather than a cold blue-white, and avoid coloured bulbs – they always look cheap.

NIGHTLIGHTS

Extra twinkle comes from masses of nightlights sheltered from the wind in jam jars – dot them around the garden in the beds and borders. You'll come to a natural stop when you can't bear to light any more or have run out of jam jars.

PAPER LANTERNS

I like to make lanterns from take-away style paper bags (chop off the handles). Use 10cm or so of sand to weigh down the bag, then nestle a nightlight in among it. You can also buy paper lanterns with

Scent

We often focus all our attention on the visual aspects of homemaking, but scent can have as much impact on your frame of mind as lighting or colour. It can totally alter the atmosphere and feel of a space. Use fragrance to create different moods and effects. Just as we wear perfume, our homes can wear many fragrances.

ESSENTIALS OILS

I use essential oils every day to fragrance my home as an alternative to scented candles. They work out less expensive and allow me to make blends to suit my mood. There are plenty of ways to use them – a few drops in the water of an oil burner, or on a ring diffuser that sits on the bulb of a light fitting (see right). I also use essential oils on anything that 'soaks it up' and will hold the fragrance, anything from tissues, cotton wool balls to unfinished wood or unglazed ceramic will work. Oils are also a great refresh for herbal sachets – just a few drops is needed every month or so. In short, they're a great all-rounder and I couldn't be without them. Fragrance, like pretty much everything else in your home, is personal. I've put together a collection of oils that suit me (I see many of them as an extension of my medicine cupboard as we also use them to cure minor ailments). My favourites are lavender, for refreshing lavender bags, for making home-made linen waters and for applying to minor burns. Neroli absolute and frankincense are my all-time favourites for the oil burner. They're perfect day or night. Then there's geranium, a great substitute for the vastly expensive rose otto oil.

SCENTED CANDLES

Good-quality candles fill a room with a fragrance that is delightful rather than artificial or sickly sweet. Use natural beeswax for dining, as the honeyed, natural scent won't overpower the food. (See page 130 for more about candles).

POTPOURRI

Personally, I can't love dried potpourri. Just thinking about it makes me want to sneeze. Those skimpy little bowls of wrinkly bits and bobs always seem a little sad to me, as if they're sucking the energy out of a room. They're also an absolute dust magnet. Bunches of dried seedpods or flowerheads, or chunky bundles of dried lavender piled high in an oversized bowl are the way to go in my view. An alternative is rock-salt potpourri – it doesn't attract so much dust and so is a great alternative for those prone to allergies (see right).

ROOM AND LINEN SPRAYS

Giving a room a quick spritz with a room spray is an instant pick-me-up. I keep a bottle on the landing and use it a couple of times as I walk past during the day. I prefer to be able to refresh the scent when I want rather than having a constant background scent. And as part of my morning routine, I use a linen spray on my sheets.

THE PROJECT
Make your own scented candles

Scented candles can be expensive, but it's quite easy to make your own. I save all the leftover bits of wax from my candles and add them to new shop-bought wax pellets.

YOU'LL NEED:

✳ A double boiler. It's worth buying one (from specialist craft shops) if you're going to be making candles regularly. Otherwise melt the wax bain-marie style, in a large bowl over a pan of boiling water.
✳ Wax. The quantity depends on the size and number of candles you're planning to make.
✳ Paper or metal-cored wicks of the correct thickness for the containers you will be using. Your craft supplier can advise you on the correct size to ensure the wick burns and the wax melts evenly.
✳ Wick sustainers. These hold the wick in place.
✳ A range of moulds. I re-use glass containers from old candles. Teacups and small thick-glassed tumblers are all suitable too.
✳ Essential oils. These are used to scent the candle.

HOW TO:

✳ Melt the wax using the double boiler or in a bowl over boiling water.
✳ Prepare the wick by crimping the sustainer to one end of the wick, dipping it in the melted wax and setting it aside to dry.
✳ Dip the sustainer in the melted wax again so that it sticks to the bottom of the mould. Make sure that it's in the centre. Leave to dry.
✳ Place a pencil horizontally across the top of the mould and twist the loose end of the wick around it to keep the wick upright. Be careful not to pull the wick out of the sustainer.
✳ If you are scenting the candle, add the essential oils to the wax now. Don't add more than 20 drops per 200g as it will affect the burn of the candle.
✳ Pour the wax into the mould and leave to set for half an hour. A small dip or well may form as the wax cools and contracts.
✳ Re-melt some wax and fill up the well, scratching the surface of the set wax first with a pin. Your candle will be ready to burn the next day. Trim the wick before lighting.

ESSENTIAL OILS
For very little expense, you can put together a scent 'wardrobe' for your home using the essential oils that appeal to you personally.

You don't actually need any specialist kit to use essential oils in your home. A few drops of lavender oil on a tissue slipped into your pillowcase will help you sleep. In winter, dab a few drops of oil onto a damp cloth and place it on a warm radiator to scent the room. I use essential oils on anything that will soak it up, whether it's a piece of unglazed ceramic (like the flower on my bedside), or unsealed wood, like the wooden hearts (originally christmas tree decorations), that scent my wardrobe.

A NON-DUSTY POT POURRI ALTERNATIVE?
Add a few drops of essential oil to a cup full of rock salt. Refresh every few weeks with more oil and a stir of the salt.

SPRAY
consider the method of application of scent as much as the scent itself. Room spray is instant, light – perfect for spring and summer.

It takes no time at all and it's the next best thing to getting that 'just-laundered' feeling when you slide into bed at night. (Also see page 47 for how to make your own ironing water.)

You can use linen sprays to scent your towels too. I also love the clever trick of spraying napkins with a spritz of linen spray. The smell is subtle and doesn't overpower the food; you just catch a whiff when you bring your napkin to your mouth.

INCENSE

It doesn't have to smell all hippy-dippy. Things have moved on and you can now get clean, sophisticated scents in a variety of sizes of sticks and cones for use both indoors and out.

REED DIFFUSERS

These oils with reed sticks are a very popular way to fragrance a room. They are great value for money and you don't have to worry about naked flames.

SCENTED SACHETS AND BAGS

Lavender is the obvious choice for a scented sachet. I made several refillable linen bags a few years ago – just a small rectangle stitched on three sides with an open top tied with a length of ribbon. I refill these each summer with a fresh batch of dried lavender.

FLOWERS, FOLIAGE AND HOUSE PLANTS

With many of our shop-bought flowers so often devoid of fragrance it's easy to forget just how powerful the scent of some flowers can be. A vase of sweet peas, a few stems of perfumed garden roses or a small posy of lily-of-the-valley will gently fragrance a whole room. It's not just flowers that are scented though. Many aromatic herbs release their fragrance when you brush against them or stroke their leaves. Dill and fennel with their aniseed scent, and eucalyptus are all energising and uplifting. I bring the scented pelargoniums in from the garden to my office to overwinter, so I can stroke the rose-scented leaves of Pelargonium 'Attar of Roses' when I'm at my desk.

Too much of a good thing

✳ Don't overdo it – you can have too much of a good thing. Learn to be subtle. And remember that your house will have a smell of its own – leather chairs, waxed floors, furniture polish. The things you surround yourself with all help create the particular fragrance of your home.

✳ Never put heady, strongly scented flowers in the bedroom. They can end up disturbing your sleep.

✳ When adding scent, take into account the strength of the fragrance in relation to the size of the room. A large three-wick candle would be too much in a downstairs loo or a small bedroom, but would be perfect in a roomy lounge.

✳ It's good to alter the fragrance, to alter the mood. Sometimes it's good not to add anything fragranced to give your nose a rest.

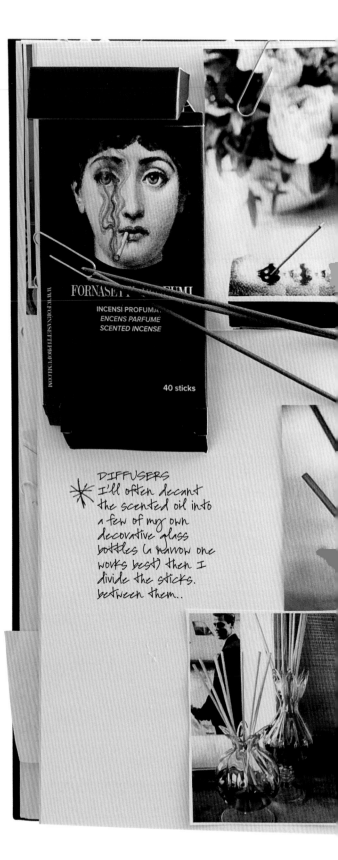

✳ DIFFUSERS
I'll often decant the scented oil into a few of my own decorative glass bottles (a narrow one works best) then I divide the sticks between them..

...ENSE
...hink the key to
...ense is to burn
...where there's a
...the breeze from
...open window or
... – it will help
...ry the scent;
...also prevent
...from becoming
... overpowering. I
... to use incense
... in the garden
...much as I do
...oors. I love the
... it gently wafts
... the house.

NO-SEW SCENTING FOR WARDROBES AND LINENS
Keep your prettiest lavender bags out on show, and
make simple sachets for the wardrobe – simply cut
squares of muslin or cotton, place a spoon of lavender
in the middle, draw up the edges and tie with ribbon.
Soap wrapped in tissue will also do the trick.

SCENTED FLOWERS & PLANTS
Natural fragrance and beauty
– a perfect partnership. It's
also a way of marking the
milestones of the year. To me,
narcissi means spring is on its
way, while lilac and sweetpeas
tell me that summer's just
beginning. Enjoy those fleeting
moments and fill a vase with a
flower whilst it's in season.

Seductive & uplifting

✳ Light, subtle florals are great all-rounders; a few drops of rose otto or geranium oil which lift any room without overpowering.
✳ Heady, sweet seductive florals suit the bedroom, but use them sparingly – just a single stem of tuberose, hyacinth or jasmine or a couple of drops of neroil or rose otto oil on a burner is enough.
✳ Heady florals are often combined beautifully with woody, oriental and spicey notes in scented candles – perfect for the winter months in the living room.

Understanding Scent

Scent is a crucial part of creating 'home'. Fragrances lift your spirit, adding layers of mood and memory to the emotional blueprint of the home, but how do you choose your scent?

Warming & comforting

✳ Vanilla is sweet, relaxing and sensuous and is perfect for the lounge or the bedroom. The more subtle, less overpowering honeyed notes of beeswax candles are perfect the dining table.
✳ Spicey aromas such as cinnamon, clove and nutmeg combine well together and create the classic Christmas combo when mixed with orange – great for the kitchen or the lounge.
✳ These fragrances come into their own in the colder months – use them where you want to create a warm cosy atmosphere.

Fresh & reviving

✳ You can't help but associate lemon and pine with kitchens – they scream 'clean', but they work equally well in the bathroom, along with mint and grapefruit as they are all invigorating.

✳ Aromatics like rosemary and eucalyptus are stimulating and can aid concentration – making them perfect for the office.

✳ Lavender will help you sleep, but in larger doses it becomes reviving and of course is one of the best ways to keep bedlinen and towels smelling fresh.

Rich & moody

✳ The burning embers of a fire, the scent of furniture polish and leather, damp moss on a shady wall all shout 'autumn'.

✳ These moody, smokey, musky smells evoke a certain mood – a little darker, a little more mysterious – the opposite of light and airy florals. They work best in candles and incense form.

✳ Use aromatic oils from the resins frankincense, myrrh and amber to create the same intimacy and warmth. All these fragrances work best in living areas of the home.

Household smrells

Now that open-plan living is so popular, the smells created by activities such as cooking that were once restricted to one area of the house may well filter through to others. These aromas, and many others, can permeate spaces where you would rather live without them.

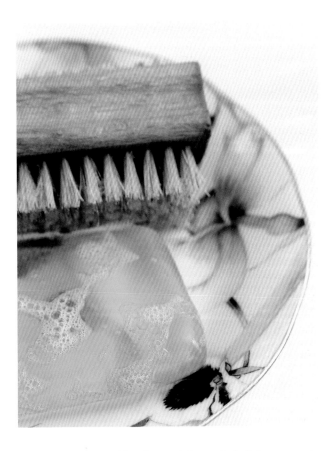

GETTING RID OF THE SMELLS YOU DON'T WANT

Lighting a couple of furtively placed scented candles isn't going to disguise the multitude of accumulated stale smells in your house. Here are my tips for dealing with them:

✳ A clean house smells clean. Spending money on expensive candles, or worse, on proprietary air fresheners and fabric fresheners, is fruitless unless your house is clean to start with. Establish old-fashioned spring-cleaning rituals – airing duvets, washing pillows and comforters each year, beating rugs and cushions every few months. Just because something doesn't look dirty doesn't mean it's clean. Smell it and you'll know.

✳ You may be desensitised to how your home smells. There's your own smell and that of other members of the family to consider, as well as the smell of beloved family pets. Plus any smells of damp or mould need to be hunted back to source and tackled urgently.

✳ Air your house on a regular basis – it will stop the build-up of stale smells and won't give them a chance to linger.

✳ Before you go on holiday, clean and change the bed, tidy up, empty bins and empty the fridge. That way you won't be welcomed home by any unpleasant odours.

✳ To help get rid of stale cooking smells, simmer a pan of water to which you've added some lemon juice (for more spring-cleaning ideas, see pages 118–119).

✳ Bicarbonate of soda is a good natural de-odouriser for fabrics. Sprinkle onto the area and leave for 15mins to an hour before brushing or hoovering off.

✳ If you have a problem with odours that linger in your fridge, even after you've given it a good clear out – place a few pieces of charcoal on a saucer in the fridge – it will absorb the smell.

✳ Everyday products smell too!

The washing-up liquid you use at the kitchen sink, the fabric softener you use for your laundry, the floor cleaner, the glass cleaner – all these simple everyday products add their own fragrance to your home. Be aware and buy with care.

*Shop around for your flowers – just as you would anything else. It's fine to pick up a bunch from the supermarket (many are now supporting local growers, which is great) and mix it with a few stems of something really special from a florists. Search out your local grower too. Many 'pick your own' fruit farms have diversified and now grow cut flowers. They can offer amazing value.

The basic flower arranger's kit

I tend not to do complex flower arrangements at home as I prefer things to be much freer and more natural, so I don't need anything more than a basic kit. My wedding- and party-styling kit is another matter though. Here's what I think you'll find useful in your home:

✳ Scissors – kept sharp and clean.

✳ A sharp knife to cut tough flower stems cleanly. Jagged edges encourage bacteria, which will kill off your flowers quicker.

✳ Secateurs for when the scissors and knife aren't man enough for the job. They're essential for cutting woody stems.

✳ A stem and thorn stripper. This is a hand-held tool that removes foliage and thorns quickly. Not essential (the job's just as easily done with a gloved hand and a grimace), but useful if you've got a lot of flowers, for instance if you're styling for a party or a friend's wedding.

✳ String for tying up bouquets. Wire is easier for tying harder woody stems, but if you're using wire, you'll need wire cutters – don't just blunt the scissors or secateurs.

✳ For wrapping bouquets, potted plants or herbs as presents, I have a cupboard full of ribbons, wrapping papers, cellophane, hessian and tissue paper. It's amazing what a little 'dressing' can do.

✳ 'Flower frogs' – also called pin holders – usually consisting of brass pins set into a lead base. These are a good alternative to using floral foam and will help prevent flowers from leaning out to the sides and leaving a hole in the middle of an arrangement. Buy the size that suits you and your favourite vases. I find 5cm and 10cm the most useful. Use waterproof florist's tack (with the texture of putty) to stick it to the base of the vase.

Flowers

Flowers are joyful. Just the simple gesture of positioning a tumbler or jam jar with a few daffodils picked from the garden can be enough to bring life into a room, show it is cared for, considered and loved.

But...flowers can represent so much more than that. They are with us along the way, helping us mark the highs and lows of life. They are linked with emotions and ritual, from the everyday to the major rights of passage – in courtship, friendship, marriage, birth and death. Flowers dignify us, and our homes.

FOUR TIPS FOR BUYING FLOWERS

1 A good florist cares for their flowers. Buckets will be topped up regularly with fresh water and positioned carefully away from draughts from doors and windows, air-conditioning units and heaters. Flowers will be shaded from full sun and will be moved from outside on a hot summer's day to the cool of indoors. All this TLC is to prolong the life of the flowers. If the bucket you lift your flowers from is dry or you can feel the blast from the industrial heater above as you reach to grab them, leave them well alone.

2 Flowers should look fresh and pert and the leaves should be green and healthy, avoid any with yellowing or fading foliage.

3 In general, avoid buying flowers that have lots of pollen on the petals. It's a sure sign that they're past their best.

4 Try to buy local and seasonal flowers whenever possible. It makes common sense, but above all, buy flowers that make you smile.

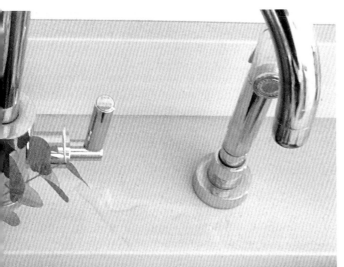

Give your flowers a little TLC

Florists 'condition' the flowers they sell to prolong vase life. You can use some of the same tricks to extend the life of your bought blooms.

＊ Before arranging your flowers, cut 2.5cm off the stem on the diagonal. This gives a larger surface area for the flower to drink water and will stop the stem from sitting flat on the bottom of the vase where it won't be able to absorb as much water. To keep bacteria at bay, cut off any leaves that will sit below the water.

＊ Some flowers release a milky sap. To stop this happening, 'sear' the bottom of their stems by holding them above a flame from a lighter, or the ring on a gas hob for a few seconds.

＊ Don't just fling the sachet of flower food in the bin. Use it, it works! Most commercial flower foods contain a sugar for nourishment, an acid to help soak up the water, and a bleach or anti-bacterial agent to keep bacteria at bay.

＊ Any bacteria that's lurking in a vase could shorten the life span of your flowers. Use a little bleach or baby sterilising liquid and hot water to thoroughly clean the vase before use.

＊ Keep an eye on the water levels, and top up frequently (every day or so) – change it completely if it looks cloudy at all. When this happens, I also take the stems out and rinse them under a running tap before putting them back in the vase to keep bacteria at bay.

＊ Pull out any fading flowers as the days go by to prolong the life of the others in the bunch. I also cut an inch or so more off the stems, especially on roses when the bottoms of the stems go black.

＊ Flowers will last longer in a cool room than in a warm one. During winter, when the heating is on in the house, I move my displays to a cooler part of the house overnight – somewhere like a north-facing windowsill, a porch or an unheated conservatory. It means I'll get a couple more days out of the display.

＊ Keep your flowers away from fruit. In the same way that a ripe banana will ripen green tomatoes from the garden, it will 'ripen' your flowers too.

Make your own flower food

Add two tablespoons of white vinegar, two tablespoons of sugar and a teaspoon of household bleach to two pints of warm water and use as your flower water. Increase or decrease the amounts depending on the size of your vase.

Flower arranging without any preconceptions

Teacups and jugs, vintage china and glass, wood and metal bowls – nearly every type of vessel can be used as a vase, including milk bottles, jam jars and old tin cans.

NOT A VASE

A vase doesn't have to be a 'vase'. Pretty much anything can be used to hold flowers, even if it's not waterproof. You just need to pop a waterproof container inside – a tumbler or a plastic water bottle with its top cut off will do the trick. Old favourites can be brought into service – chipped or cracked jugs, cups, mugs or urns that still look beautiful but aren't watertight can be given new life. Your 'vase' collection will double instantly, as you start eyeing up pretty cardboard boxes as a viable option for a vase.

NOT A FLOWER

Set aside any preconceptions about what it is you think you should be putting in a vase. Flowers don't have to be 'flowers' all the time. You don't always need a dozen roses, a bunch of five hyacinths or a wrap of lilies. There's beauty in an armful of Acer leaves cut just as their autumn colours are beginning to show or in a tangle of hedgerow bramble picked before the fruit has ripened. Its green berries flushed with pink are a joy to behold. A good florist should be able to track down suppliers of the more interesting stock. If not, it's time to hunt on your own.

Three things to consider when making a vase collection

1 Think of the style, size, shape and natural habit of the kinds of flowers you like to use most, and how you like to arrange them. Do you buy a bunch of long-stemmed stargazer lilies for the hall table every two weeks? A tall vase that widens at the top will maximize their impact. Do you snip garden roses for the bedside? Think short and sweet. Buy vases for practicality as well as style.

2 Consider the size and scale of the vase. If it's not in constant use, where will you store it? You may be better off investing in a large decorative vase or jug that will look just as good without flowers so that it can be displayed while being 'stored'.

3 Every 'vase' – a teapot, an urn or a plain glass vase – gives off a style message, as do the flowers inside it. Use this to show off your personal style. Choose the flowers you are drawn to and carefully select the vase that marries (or contrasts) with it best. Have fun. This is one of the most creative and enjoyable parts of homemaking.

*I have a bit of a thing about white pitchers and jugs – for me, they make the perfect vase. I've got over twenty now. Starting a collection like this gives you a theme to work towards. It makes your selection more focused and less of a jumble, and it means they'll look just as good without flowers in them at all.

RAID THE GARDEN

Head out into the garden, scissors or secateurs in hand and experiment with flowers and foliage that you like the look of. If you're a keen gardener, you may already be growing plenty of plants that would make suitable cut material, such as old-fashioned garden roses, mop head hydrangeas, camellias and hellebores.

A few snipped every now and then won't leave your garden bare. Cutting your own foliage is a great way to pad out a shop-bought bunch. A few trails of jasmine or ivy, or a couple of branches of blossom will add a home-grown feel. If you can't bring yourself to cut flowers from your beds and borders just before their prime, why not plant a dedicated cutting garden in part of your garden?

Don't overlook the little ones

Shorter flowers from the garden don't normally get a look in when thinking of flowers to arrange – miniature spring bulbs, muscari, daffodils, snowdrops, for example, go unpicked because of their diminutive size, but these flowers are exactly the flowers that are best appreciated up close and personal. Shot glasses, espresso cups and eggcups all make perfect receptacles. Position them where you'll be able to gaze upon them at their level – the bedside table, the bath surround. It's also a great way to use up any flowering arranging or gardening casualties – the lily flower that snaps off when you're unwrapping the bunch or the rose that's decapitated by a football in the garden and breaks off an inch below the flower head.

*Cluster short-stemmed beauties together in groups for more impact, and raid the kitchen cupboards for suitably-sized 'vases'. Anything goes – even jam jars can be made to look chic when tied together with ribbon to form a centrepiece.

Flower arranging magic

Arranging flowers is one of the most enjoyable parts of homemaking. Trust yourself and your 'eye' – and have fun. Arrangements don't have to be formal in any way. Even the simple act of putting a few stems into a jam jar lifts a space.

SIMPLE IS GOOD
A display made from masses of one type of flower looks generous and is simple to achieve. If you're at all worried about what goes with what, this is the one for you. Save money by buying in season and shopping at the market rather than the corner florist.

POTTED PLANTS RULE
Potted plants can flower for weeks, even months, so they can offer fantastic value for money, especially if you're after a large-scale display. Probably the most common is the orchid, then at Christmas time, the poinsettia. You can be quite decadent and not even plant them up, but just nestle them, still in their plastic pots in a big container or bowl and use moss to conceal what's going on. Most plants will survive perfectly well like this for the duration of flowering and you can lavish them with a bit of TLC when you take them out of the spotlight.

Don't overlook potted plants as cutting material for your arrangements. Sometimes they're the only way to get the flowers you really want at the time you want them. It can make great financial sense too. Once you've cut the flowers you're left with the plant to grow on in the garden if it's not tender, or to nurse back into flowers indoors if it is. I've done this with plenty of plants over the years, but mostly regularly with hydrangeas, lily-of-the-valley and hellebores.

THE FOLIAGE IS JUST AS IMPORTANT AS THE FLOWERS
Foliage isn't just about padding out a bouquet, it's about adding extra interest to an arrangement, bringing in varying heights, shapes, textures and colours as well as additional fragrance. Twisting trails of jasmine, the fluffy, stroke-able texture of lamb's ears (Stachys), the fresh and uplifting scent of mint – all bring something special to a bunch. Choose foliage with as much consideration as you would flowers. An armload of silver-grey large-leafed eucalyptus or a few oak branches flushed with vivid green growth can be things of beauty in their own right, even when there isn't a single flower in sight.

YOU DON'T NEED MASSES
Quanity isn't everything. A vase doesn't need to be full. A bunch of flowers embellished with ribbon and arranged within a larger vase looks sculptural and much 'bigger' than the flowers themselves.

Common flower-arranging problems
✳ Flowers that are splaying out to the edge of the vase, leaving a hole in the middle? Use a flower frog (see page 142) or criss-cross sellotape across the mouth of the container, then place the stems in between. The sellotape holds the stems in place and is normally hidden by the foliage and flowers.
✳ Roses that have flopped? Cut a little off the stems at a diagonal, then place in a mug or jug of boiling water for thirty seconds, taking care not to steam the flower heads. Place back into cold water. This should revive them if you got to them early enough.
✳ Flowers that are cut too short? Re-use the cellophane they came in, crumpled at the bottom of the vase to elevate them.

02
the colour palette

HOW DO YOU REACT TO COLOUR?
WHICH COLOURS AFFECT YOU JOYFULLY, WHICH NEGATIVELY?
UNDERSTANDING HOW COLOUR CONTRASTING WITH IT.
THE KEY IS TO HARMLY COHARMING WITH IT.

*Think about the bigger picture – it isn't just about the vase and the flowers itself. Where and how you position the vase counts. Try somewhere a little different or place it off-centre. Bring in other elements – such as multiple vases, postcards, candles or books to expand the display.

MULTIPLE CHOICE

Cluster single stems of one type of flower in a collection of mismatched bottles, tumblers, jam jars or any small container that's suitable. Alternatively, keep the containers uniform and mix up the flowers. Placing one flower per vase like this makes a few stems go much further and gives your final display more impact. The trick is to keep to a theme or style (cottage-like, say), or a colour or flower type (yellow and white or spring bulbs) to stop it from looking too bitty.

GO SOLO

Sometimes it only takes one, single perfect bloom to take centre stage. Depending on the time of year (and my particular fancy at that moment), it could be a camellia from my garden – a perfectionist flower, with its orderly arrangement of petals – or one of my favourite roses, 'Yves Piaget', which has the archetypal rose fragrance that one expects, but rarely ges with shop-bought roses. I chop the stem brutally short, pop the flower in a simple glass tumbler from the kitchen cupboard, and put it at my bedside table.

How to make your Phalaenopsis orchid bloom again

Cut back the stem to the base of the plant. Keep the orchid in a cool room (around 12°C) with plenty of light for a period of about 4 weeks to stimulate the flower spike production. Then move to somewhere a little warmer (16°C). Orchids like to dry out in between watering (but not for too long), so on average, water once a week, depending on the conditions in your home. Use rainwater rather than tap water as they don't like lime. Feeding with a high-potash fertiliser will encourage flowers to form.

Forcing Blossom

It's possible to cut stems from flowering shrubs and trees like magnolia and cherry blossom whilst still in bud and force them into flower much earlier than their natural period in the warmer conditions of your home.

✳ Look for thin stems – they are easier to force than thick ones. Buds need to be fat and plump – so don't cut too early.

✳ Make a upturned 'V' shape cut at the bottom of the stem – to soak up the most water.

✳ Place the stems in a cool place first (10ºC), like a porch/unheated conservatory before bringing into the warmer rooms of the house.

✳ It should then take about a week to ten days for the flowers to open. Mist the stems every so often to stop the petals drying out and becoming brown.

Tricking nature

You will probably have seen, if not bought, some of those almost ready-to-flower potted spring bulbs for indoors in shops a good couple of months or so before they make an appearance 'real-time' in our gardens.

You may even have potted up your own specially prepared bulbs in late autumn and started the process yourself from scratch. If you haven't you should, as indoor bulbs offer great-value displays for minimal effort and after flowering can be planted in your garden (they will flower again though they won't be quite as showy in the years to come). But it's not just spring bulbs that you can trick – or 'force' into flowering early by bringing indoors.

Ideas for quick floral presents

PLANTS IN POTS
Potted plants such as miniature roses, orchids, hydrangeas and pots of spring or summer bulbs all make perfect presents. Rather than buy an outer pot (who wants all those mismatched pots anyway?), use fabric to dress the one it came in. Hessian can be bought in bulk online and gives pots a natural rustic feel that works with most plants, but use any square of fabric you happen to have that you like the look of. Position the pot in the middle, draw the fabric up around it and tie in place with ribbon, a piece of leather thong or string.

IN A JAR
Fill a jam jar or Kilner jar with flowers – ideally scented – picked from the garden. Dress it up with a length of ribbon tied around the neck. Homegrown flowers like this are delicate and don't travel well; keeping them in water like this is the best way to go.

EDIBLE TREATS
Mix in some edibles where you can – lemon verbena and mint for tea, herbs to cook with, or edible flowers to add to a salad.

ONLY HERBS
A herb-only bouquet makes a useful gift to friends you're staying with. Treat them as you would flowers and keep them in water; delicate herbs like dill, fennel, basil and lemon balm all wilt quickly.

THE PROJECT
Forcing lily-of-the-valley

The appearance of lily-of-the-valley (Convallaria majalis) in the garden, which flowers in mine in late May, marks the transition from spring to summer, but it's possible to make it bloom indoors in just three to four weeks. The delicate bell-shaped white flowers give off the most stunningly sweet floral fragrance – it's known as muguet and is highly prized in the world of perfume. A small bunch will scent a whole room.

HOW TO:
✳ Most mail-order companies send out the dormant rhizomes in late winter. Plant them straight away when they arrive. Each piece should have at least one 'pip' – a pointy white growing tip.
✳ Before planting, trim about 1cm off the roots. This will kick-start them into growing and will help them take up moisture.
✳ Soak the pips in lukewarm water for a few hours in a bowl or your sink.
✳ Fill your container of choice with a loam-based compost, at least 10cm deep. You don't need to bother with crocks or drainage.
✳ Plant the pips about 5cm apart so that just the tips show. They look great planted en masse in a bulb bowl, but look just as special three or five to a small container. Water well.
✳ Place the pot in a cool bright area, but away from direct sunlight. Water when the surface of the soil feels dry to the touch.
✳ Once they've flowered, you can plant them in the garden. Don't cut the leaves; allow them to die naturally to nourish the plant for the following year.

*Why force something? There's a certain thrill to be had in getting hold of something prerelease – flowers are no different. Nearing the end of a long winter, any signal that tells me spring is on its way is welcome in my house.

PIECING TOGETHER THE JIGSAW

the
HALLWAY

The entrance hallway is the first and last thing you experience when you arrive and leave your home. Doubtless, it is primarily a functional area, easing the transition from the outdoors to in. It is used as a place to store coats, shoes, boots, brollies, prams and trikes. It is also a place that links and leads to the other areas of the home. It is the introduction. It is where visitors linger to say their goodbyes, where the delivery man waits while you sign for a package. Your hallway gives you a chance to set the tone and mood of your home.

For these reasons, the hallway is one of the most exciting of spaces. Frequently undervalued and neglected, it is often treated as the poor relation to the living room or dining room. In fact, your hallway is your first impression, your welcome and your opportunity to show the world something of yourself. The hallway has to work hard as a high traffic area, and unless you are fantastically minimalist there is little you can do to avoid it housing the inevitable and necessary possessions of family life. However, by installing practical solutions and using a little imagination, your hallway can become a place of joy. Whatever its size or dimension, treat it as a room in itself – a gallery space, a library, and if there is room, a place to position a chair and read a book. Use mirrors, pictures, photographs, colour and carpet to warm and nurture this most important of spaces. If you invest time in your hallway and bring it to beauty, you will always feel happy to walk in your door.

Piecing the hallway together

Space and living style will dictate how you want to use your hallway, and in turn how you choose to furnish it. Think of your hallway not only as giving the first impression of your home, but as an opportunity to make it as much of a room, or series of rooms, as any other in the house.

TABLES

Hallway tables are essential places to sort the post and keep other necessities, such as your handbag, wallet, phones and keys. As hallways are generally narrow spaces, it's important to leave at least 90cm clearance for the walkway for it to feel comfortable.

Consoles make great hallway tables. Ones that are designed with curves or an open lower half do not feel too blocky and solid, and so are perfect in small spaces. Tables made from clear materials, such as glass and acrylic, seem to 'disappear' altogether. Aim for integrated storage to hide the clutter wherever you can. Where space might not permit a table, you can fit an equally slim, cut-to-length floating shelf or series of shelves for this purpose. This would also give you the opportunity to suspend hooks from beneath the bottom shelf for the children's coats and school bags, if that is one of your requirements.

SEATING

Unless you've got masses of space, you probably won't be looking for anything other than a practical place to perch while you take your shoes off. There are many benches and other quirky styles of bench seat. Again, a shallow design is a good idea for a hallway, and many double up as storage. The aim is to keep as much order in the chaos of life's paraphernalia as possible.

Treat it like any other room

Don't feel restricted about what you can and can't bring into your hallway. From a style point of view, anything goes. There's nothing to say that a wardrobe wouldn't work as a coat cupboard in the right space or that a chest of drawers wouldn't look fabulous as a hallway 'table'. Have the confidence to use what pleases you, as well as what will provide the practical solution.

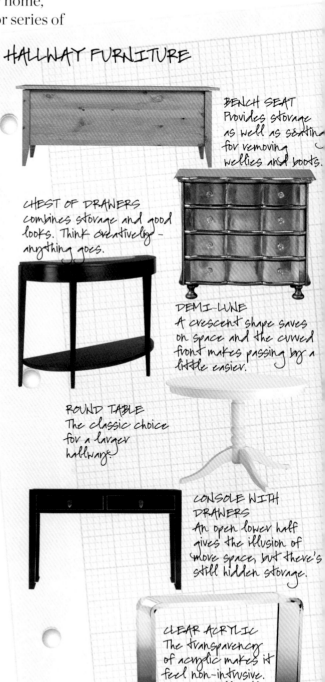

HALLWAY FURNITURE

BENCH SEAT Provides storage as well as seating for removing wellies and boots.

CHEST OF DRAWERS combines storage and good looks. Think creatively – anything goes.

DEMI-LUNE A crescent shape saves on space and the curved front makes passing by a little easier.

ROUND TABLE The classic choice for a larger hallway.

CONSOLE WITH DRAWERS An open lower half gives the illusion of more space, but there's still hidden storage.

CLEAR ACRYLIC The transparency of acrylic makes it feel non-intrusive. Use in small halls with low light levels.

Make it feel like a gallery

Instead of seeing the hallway as a pass-through space treat it more as a place to showcase you artworks and treasures. All of us have our own little collections and these can be displayed with a museum-style twist. Pictured here is an old glass cabinet that is slim enough to work on this upper landing. The trike, and type of objects keep the idea from looking too serious.

Making a good first impression

The hallway is the first room you see every day when you arrive home and it's also the first room your guests see. But all too often, its decoration is overlooked. You should therefore design and decorate this space with as much thought as you would any other room.

THE DÉCOR

The hallway and landings (if you have them) link together all the other areas of your home. Decide whether you want to treat them as a neutral space with minimal decoration that quietly takes you from one room, or as a space that stands out as a statement on its own terms – an area of colour and pattern – that then leads you to a calmer space in another room.

THE LIGHTING

Stairs need to be adequately lit plus you need to be able to reach into any hall cupboard and see exactly what's inside. The hallway though can also be a prime candidate for ambient lighting (see page 127). The minute you place a table lamp giving off a warm glow in the hallway, it immediately makes your home look and feel inviting.

The hallway is also the place to add a statement pendant light fitting. Even if you haven't got space for anything else in the hall, you'll probably have room for a decorative light fitting. Choose one that looks good from all angles, including from the top of the stairs.

HALLWAY 'VIEWS'

Many doors connect to and from a hallway or landing. While the view from the front door is probably the most important, and the one we all think of first, there are others to consider too. Think about the view out to the hallway from inside the lounge, or the 'look through' from an open-plan kitchen diner. Try your best to create a pleasing view, perhaps by using a strategically placed artwork or papering a section of a wall. Think about the view from the stairs too. As you look down, is there something beautiful to attract your eye, such as a statement light fitting or an unusual dainty table?

MAKING THE HALL FEEL BIGGER

Hallways and landings are often narrow, tight and dark spaces. Choosing a light neutral colour for the walls and floor will help to make them feel more roomy, as will framing artwork in light-coloured frames. In a really tight space, opt for narrow picture frames that project from the wall – every little extra space counts.

Mirrors are your best friends in a narrow hallway; they trick the eye into believing the space is much bigger. Choose the largest wall-hung mirror that you can fit in or even consider removing the skirting boards and covering one whole wall with a floor-to-ceiling mirror.

FRAGRANCE AND FLOWERS

The hallway offers an opportunity to say 'welcome', create a certain mood or set the scene for a party through your use of fragrance and flowers. Warming scents, such as spicy florals and vanilla are inviting – a room diffuser or spray is best, as it's not a good idea to leave candles or oil burners unattended. A vase of flowers is always a lovely touch. If you do fake flowers, the hallway is the place for them. People don't tend to eye things up for too long in the hall; they would have moved on to another room before they have realised the flowers are fake. For the illusion to work, do keep the fakes seasonal.

SOFTENING IT UP

A doormat is a practical addition to any hall. If you haven't got sufficient clearance between the door and the floor for a traditional brush mat, try a flat-weave runner as an alternative. Choose one that can be thrown in the washing machine so it's easy to maintain. Any rugs and runners need to be well secured, so use a non-slip mat underneath. If you have particularly cold winters, think about fitting a door curtain made from a thick heavy fabric; I'm always amazed at just how much warmer the hall is with one of these curtains. There's also something quite special about being able to draw the curtains on the outside world for the night.

WAYS TO ADD INTEREST TO A HALLWAY

WALLPAPER
Is there a pattern you love but aren't brave enough to use in the living room or bedroom? Think about using it in the hallway instead. You'll still get the pleasure of seeing it, and it will be much easier to live with in a space that you generally use to pass through.

ACCESSORIZE
Bring in a large wall-hung mirror and an ornate chandelier to add a decorative touch if there isn't room for furniture.

PAINT
A strong wall colour gives the hall it's own identity. Painting the floors white prevents the space from being too dark.

A CARPET RUNNER
Patterned or plain, it's the simplest way to make a statement.

PATTERNED RISERS
Make a feature of the risers (the uprights) by painting them with a pattern or a simple decorative motif. Wallpaper can also be used just as effectively.

A RIBBON OF COLOUR
Use floor paint to create a faux runner on uncarpeted stairs. This should be done with great precision so it reads well to the eye.

Easing the transition between inside and out

The small journey from the outside to the inside of a home is important and should be ideally governed by a sense of serenity, order and calm.

This little leap frames the welcome to your home, and a barrage of possessions, clothes and junk can easily undermine this sentiment.

DEALING WITH THE CLUTTER

The hallway can quickly become a dumping ground. This is hard to avoid; it is a working space that has to bear a lot of traffic. However, giving up on it and allowing it to gradually become ungovernable is a mistake. Be mindful and incorporate adequate storage, putting in a system that will nip clutter problems in the bud.

✳ Coats, jackets, bags, wellies and all other outer clothing need a home; otherwise you will pile them on top of the bannister or at the bottom of the stairs. If you haven't got a space for a separate cloakroom, try to squeeze a coat cupboard in somewhere on the ground floor. A built-in fixture is best, but even a freestanding wardrobe (without too much ornate detailing so it doesn't look to bedroomy) will help. See opposite for more ideas on cloakroom.

✳ Stow away any out-of-season items somewhere else to reduce clutter. Tennis rackets, cricket bats, fishing kit or golf clubs all fall into this category.

✳ If there's space in the front garden think about installing a waterproof lockable storage chest for trikes, scooters or prams.

✳ Having somewhere to sort and deal with the post is common sense. Keep a wastepaper basket in the hall to deal with junk mail. Better still, stop it from coming through the letterbox in the first place by fixing a 'no junk mail' sign to your door or gate.

✳ Spare some room to put your keys (well out of eyeline of the door or letterbox). Also, a bowl, jar or bottle for coins may work for you.

✳ Use the backdoor if you've got one. If there's room create a 'boot room' area to allow you to deal with muddy wellies , wet dogs and dirty boots. To prevent rows of shoes lining up put a rule in place that they can't live downstairs for more than a day – move them to their proper home (upstairs in a wardrobe) as soon as they've had a day to air.

✳ Keep a box or a basket near the bottom of the stairs where all the bits and bobs that need returning upstairs can live. Encourage all family members to check this at the end of a day.

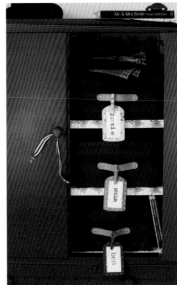

Create a mini cloakroom area

✳ You need a coat stand or a series of coat hooks on which to hang coats. If you have young children, place a second row lower down the wall so they are able to hang and retrieve their coats themselves.

✳ Try and squeeze in a small cupboard with closed storage space that can also double as a tabletop to hold a tray for coins, glasses, phones, etc. One that allows you to also store shoes underneath would be better still.

✳ A mirror will add an element of decoration and make the space feel bigger, but it's also good to know you're looking respectable before you go out into the world.

✳ If you have pets keep a lint roller or clothes brush here.

7 ways to get the most from your hall or landing

Keep your ideas practical and unfussy and you will find that there are many ways to utilise landings and hallways.

1 Landings can provide a practical solution as overflow storage for bedrooms. Seasonal clothes that you don't need for months of the year on end – such as winter woolies in the summer can be stored in a chest of drawers. Anything that does not quite fit comfortably in your wardrobe can be stored in a chest or trunk. Pop a vase on top, a few books and it all looks purposefully arranged.

2 The landing makes a good home for a linen cupboard, as this space is generally close to all the bedrooms (giving easy access for changing the beds). Built-in storage can be made to accommodate the depth you need. If you are doing this, it makes sense to try and incorporate a laundry basket, especially if you are short on space in the bathroom.

3 It is easy to create an extra 'room' on a landing – a chaise longue or comfortable chair will encourage people to really use that space, especially if you add a floor lamp (this takes less space) and a small side table to take coffee, wine and a book.

4 Some hallways and landings provide the perfect opportunity for a walk-through library – maximise the space you have with a built-in design. (See page 80 for more ideas on libraries).

5 You can make a part of your landing or hall into an exciting focal point – one wall at the end of a corridor or landing that is in a bright paint colour or papered in a pattern or hung with an artwork are all excellent, tried-and-tested ideas.

*Hallways and landings make the perfect walk-through library – and this frees up valuable wall space elsewhere in your home. Built-in bookshelves are best as you'll get the most out of every last inch. Floor to ceiling shelves are ideal, but in a narrow space this might not be possible. Instead consider the walls above head height. Could they take a shelf of books?

6 Landings are blessed with large expanses of wall going up, down, left and right. Use and emphasise whatever space you have by thinking in terms of clusters of pictures or of long 'lines' of artwork, painting and photographs. (See pages 72–75 for more ideas with art.)

7 Because halls can be narrow, light colours and controllable bright light are the obvious solution to making them feel more open. Large mirrors will also do the same trick. If you keep your bedroom doors shut, you allow your landings to be their own, contained spaces and they will therefore feel tidier and better ordered.

the LIVING ROOM

Living rooms are very precious spaces. Unlike in bedrooms or the kitchen, it is not practicality or function that dominates or informs here, but a wealth of softer requirements and needs. A sense of hospitality, of comfort, relaxation and warmth are what we seek to achieve within this central living space.

The living room offers so many opportunities to showcase the styles, colours, forms and patterns you love. From the sofa, to the window dressings, to the lighting and the soft furnishings, your living room affords many chances to show off your taste and really release your inner stylist.

Piecing together the living room

How do you use your living room? As a playroom, a den, a cinema room, a grown-ups modern-day drawing room, or as all of these? Even though your living room may be multi-functional, what's its main focus? Is it formal or informal? An everyday space or one used for special occasions?

The days of a matching three-piece suite are well and truly over. Instead, pick and mix furniture to suit your needs, taste and budget. Your sofa and chairs don't need to match shape-wise but they do need to be complementary in style.

When choosing your furniture, think about looks, comfort, ease of maintenance, style longevity and the feel that the piece brings to the room. Consider your family and its needs now and in the coming years. For instance, do you eat and drink in your living room? If you do, mess and spills are pretty much inevitable and if you have a young family, they're guaranteed.

THE SOFA
This is an investment piece so you need to get it right. Do you like to sprawl out on the sofa or is it going to be used for more formal entertaining? In which case it's better to have a more upright version. You need to know yourself and be practical too: if you're not the kind of person who will only plump up loose feather-filled seat cushions once a fortnight, then select a no-feather or fixed-cushion model instead.

CHAIRS
You're spoilt for choice in terms of style. When buying, the criteria are similar to when you're choosing a sofa. Comfort is of prime importance so make sure that the people who will use them regularly are comfortable in them and that they suit their stature.

KNOLE
A grand statement piece that feels cocooning. You are limited to a coffee table with this sofa.

SECTIONAL
A flexible option add or subtract seats to suit your requirements.

CHESTERFIELD
The low back allows unobstructed sightlines, which is good for openplan spaces.

CONTEMPORARY
Smart and tailored The high arms make coffee table a more practical partner.

CLASSIC
Elegant and sociable. A timeless style. The low arms allow easy access to side tables.

MODERN CLASSIC
A comfortable yet supportive style with cushioned arms.

Things to think about when buying a sofa
* TRY IT OUT: You absolutely must sit on it first.
* DEPTH: It really matters. Most modern sofas have a seat depth of around 100cm. That's perfect for lying or lounging on, but it won't be comfortable if you like to sit upright on your sofa. Go for a 90cm depth instead – otherwise you'll end up having to prop yourself up with lots of cushions.
* ACCESS: Check you'll be able to get the sofa in the house. If access is restricted, but you want big go for a sectional sofa.

The lowdown on cushion fillings

The filling of the cushions will affect not only how a sofa or upholstered chair looks but how it feels to sit on. There are low- and high-maintenance options: feather-filled seat cushions give a relaxed, laid-back feel but need constant plumping, whereas foam-filled ones don't – though you may feel that foam doesn't really cut it in the comfort stakes. A clever compromise is a cushion with a foam centre surrounded by feathers.

THE COFFEE TABLE

Of course you don't actually have to have a coffee table but I always recommend one – it's one of the most important pieces in a living room as everything circulates around it. It's the equivalent of the kitchen table. Don't think it has to be a neat square or rectangle. It doesn't even have to be a conventional coffee table; a blanket box, a trunk or even a few wooden wine crates screwed together would all be perfectly serviceable. The possibilities are endless.

I tend to oversize my coffee tables as I love piling up books and creating vignettes on them, but the classic proportion is two-thirds the width of the sofa. Don't position it too far from the sofa or chair or it won't be any use to anyone. But anything less than 45cm looks and feels cramped when you walk around it. I'm not too precious about my coffee table; I want people to put their feet up and make themselves at home so I've got a throw strategically placed on mine. See page 186 for ideas on styling your coffee table.

If space is really tight and you just can't fit one in, use a couple of occasional tables instead at the ends of the sofa. Then pull them into use when you need them.

CONSOLE TABLES

A console table looks great behind a sofa in the middle of an open-plan space as it 'anchors' it within the room. Ideally the table height should be at least 10cm below the top of the back of the sofa and about two-thirds of the width of the sofa. If your room is large or open-plan use a console to divide the space or if it already has a focal point such as a fireplace or artwork, place a console table against another wall to create a second focal point and balance the space.

A console table allows you to place a pair of lamps one on either end. Finish with a large mirror or painting on the wall behind. It sounds formulaic but the symmetry works every time. A console table also makes a great room divider, separating a lounge from a dining area or a study, for example.

SIDE TABLES

We all need somewhere to put our cup of tea or our glass of wine, somewhere to carefully stow a pair of glasses before an afternoon snooze, and this is where side tables come in. As well as being purely practical, they are also an opportunity to create a display or hold a vase or a lamp. Don't worry about them matching. I use a few stools and lacquered cubes as side tables dotted around the house – they're handy for when you need an extra seat and they're also easy to move if, like me, you like to ring the changes.

SUPERSIZED
If you have the room, go large. It's not wasted space. It'll double up as seating and a display area, as well as a table.

LOW LEVEL
A fluffy rug invites people to sit and lounge around a low-level table.

FLEXIBILITY
Forgoing a large table allows more space for low-level seating – perfect for young kids.

MULTIPLES
Create a large sectional table by joining lots of smaller tables.

CLUSTERS
A series of smaller tables allows you the freedom to move them when and where you want.

Layout tricks for the living room

The best way to arrange the layout of your living room depends on the space you have and how you intend to spend your time within it. If a room is used for more than one purpose, give yourself the flexibility of being able to move things as you need to.

THE CLASSIC ARRANGEMENT

A sofa, a coffee table and a pair of chairs is the classic arrangement, with the chairs either opposite one another or side-by-side. It still works brilliantly for any room because of the symmetry – just scale the furniture up or down accordingly.

A new take on the classic is a pair of sofas, with a pair of chairs positioned in a U-shape to provide three sides of a square. The fourth side is left open to the main focal point of the room such as a TV, a fabulous view through a window or a fireplace.

ROOM FOR MANOEUVRE

If a living room is used for more than one purpose, give yourself the flexibility of being able to move things to accommodate what's happening at the moment. Something as simple as turning a chair around to face the fire rather than the TV can change the focus of a room. Lightweight chairs that can be picked up easily or side tables, such as cubes or pouffes that double as seats, are also a good idea. Positioning furniture right up against the walls actually does the opposite and makes the room feel smaller.

SUBDIVIDING

In a large open-plan space it makes sense to subdivide the room. This can be done in a number of ways:

* A change in flooring will divide the various areas in a room. Moving from wooden boards to carpet will visually and psychologically define an area.
* In a large room, if you entertain regularly try to subdivide the room into a series of smaller 'conversation' zones so that chatting is easy. It could be as simple as pulling up an extra chair or stool to bridge a large gap between two sofas or chairs.
* Lighting is a useful way to define the different areas without any physical division. Ideally, zone the areas so that the lights are controllable independently. If you choose over-scaled fittings or extra-decorative lights, they will also 'anchor' each of the zones.
* Using low furniture will retain the views or look-throughs in a room whilst separating off an area. Choosing a piece that doesn't have a 'face', such as a daybed, a console or a low sideboard means that it can be used from either side.

'ZONE' IT
Zone areas with a rug or a large artwork. It's best to have all the furniture on the rug, but it's not vital.

LET FURNITURE 'FLOAT'
Furniture doesn't have to be against a wall. It can 'float' in the middle of the room – it's also a great way to divide a large room. If using a sofa this way, help anchor it by positioning a table behind.

NO FOCAL POINT?
A room without a focal point can leave you feeling uneasy. If there isn't a view, a fireplace or an architectural gem such as panelled wall to draw the eye you'll need to create your own to get the feel of the room right. Large artworks, or a cluster of smaller ones, a console with a pair of lamps or a section of wall painted a bold colour all work as DIY focal points.

DIVIDE THE SPACE
An open shelving unit will create a visual divide whilst still retaining an open feel.

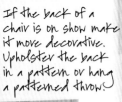

If the back of a chair is on show make it more decorative. Upholster the back in a pattern or hang a patterned throw.

USE SYMMETRY
To give a room balance appoint it with a symmetrical layout: pairs of chairs positioned opposite one another, pairs of lamps and carefully positioned pictures and mirrors all work.

*It's sometimes hard to create a living room that feels inviting and cosy in a very large room. If your ceilings are high and the proportions of the room are large, arrange the furniture so it creates a 'mini room' within the space. Cluster furniture into one area, using large-scale pieces to create impact, with a supersized sofa or an oversized floor lamp. Think big as small detailing disappears. Then use the remaining space in the room for other things – another seating area, an art installation or a library. Light all these areas separately so that at night, you can isolate the zone you're in to create an intimate environment.

Why it works: the modern day 'drawing room'

Today's living spaces are often laid out in a traditional manner, with an arrangement of two sofas and a pair of chairs making a central seating area with side tables and an ottoman or coffee table. This works both for traffic flow and for visual impact. It also leaves the edges of the room clear making the room look spacious.

FLEXIBILITY

Lightweight tables are easy to shift around the room and are especially useful for parties as you can create your own groupings. The buttoned ottoman doubles as a coffee table and an extra seating area. Its round shape makes it a perfect piece of furniture as you can sit and face any direction you like.

A PAIR OF CHAIRS

A pair of chairs allows you to alter the arrangement of the room when required. If you need to accommodate a larger standing party, move them to the sides of the room.

CREATE DIFFERENT ZONES

Treat a party room as any other multi-functional room. Each event is different, so plan for the functions and situations you need. It's a good idea to break up the space into several conversation zones (rather than just one large one). A table allows you space for games, jigsaws, etc.

'FORMAL' FURNITURE

Bear in mind that you won't always want a soft, squishy sofa. These antique pieces aren't deeply padded or cushioned so they won't be the most comfortable for watching TV, but they are perfect for when you need to sit up straight and chat. A few scatter cushions will make then a little more comfortable.

Why it works: a multi-functional living room

This is an excellent example of a living space that has also been carefully laid out to function as both a dining area, music room and a some-time office. It shows what can be done with careful planning and limited space.

DINING STYLE

The dining table in this living space is positioned in front of the window to make the most of the morning light and the view. The mismatched chairs are unified with a white paint finish – this always looks good, but here it keeps the look light and stops the chairs visually breaking the view to the window. Always consider the viewpoints of your room before buying. Here the legs of the dining table are a beautiful feature in themselves so it doesn't matter that they are seen at eye level when seated on the sofa.

IN THE ZONE

The lounge area is clearly defined and 'zoned' by way of a colourful rug. Along with the cushions it warms the room and brings in colour and pattern to an otherwise plain scheme.

MOVEABLE FEAST

Flexibility is a key part of this room's design: the small, low table is easy to move from in front of the sofa to one side (where it becomes a coffee table) to be replaced by the floor cushion, which is pulled into use when you want to lounge on the floor.

LIGHTING

The scale of the large decorative chandelier works with the proportions of the room. Its position means that it softly lights the room for dining in the evening. It works as it is backed up with task lighting (directional floor and side table lamps) that are put to use when needed.

BLANK CANVAS

The room reads as a whole and complete space because the walls and ceilings are the same soft, neutral colour. It is the colourful rug that provides the grounding for the living area and the cushions, and the art and other bright accessories add their own zest to the space as a whole. This means the room can 'breathe' and retain its airy and open quality.

THE POINTERS

There is a balance of light and dark and pattern and plain in this room: a white throw on a dark sofa; a dark throw on a white sofa; the white side table against dark sofa; the dark piano against light neutral walls. Think about achieving a balance within your scheme in relation to where you position your furniture, for both living and looks. Colourful accessories and flowers dotted throughout the room pull together and balance the brights in the scheme.

Making open plan work

So is it possible to create a room that's a bit of something for everyone? Some activities just don't go together, but that's usually due to noise (loud TV and homework, for example). In terms of utilising space though, it's just about sub-dividing the area into smaller zones. Provide sufficient table surfaces for activities that need them (or at least makeshift ones that you can have on your lap). Then ensure that everyone has the lighting they need: directional lights are best, so that others aren't disturbed whilst they're on.

Why it works: A walk-through living room

Almost a third of the floor space in this lounge is actually a walk-way between the kitchen/diner and a study at the front of the house. The goal was to design it so that the living space felt like a workable room rather than a glorified corridor.

Space savers for small rooms

✳ Large mirrors will reflect light back into the room and make it feel bigger.

✳ Keep colours light to add to the spacious feel.

✳ Opt for slimline furniture rather than pieces with oversized arms or backs with lots of padding.

✳ Sacrifice the coffee table in favour of a few occasional chairs dotted around the room.

✳ Floor lamps take up very little space. Direct them where you need the light.

CAMOUFLAGING THE TV

A wall-hung TV saves valuable wall space. By hanging pictures on the wall around the TV, it becomes less conspicuous - at first glance it blends in with the other artwork. The original fireplace (and hearth) have been removed - again, saving on valuable floor space.

SPOTLIGHT

A low, suspended ceiling light or pendant would have overpowered this room and made it feel very cramped as there just is not the volume of space for a large ceiling feature. This neat, directional multi-spotlight fitting is perfect in the space as it is tight to the ceiling, but gives flexible, directional light.

ILLUSIONARY TRICK

When this house was extended, the return window was removed and the wall-mounted mirror with its window pane design acts as a clever replacement. Below is a narrow console. Together these act as a focal point in the room, almost like a mantlepiece.

REFOCUS

Here, a corner sofa makes the most of this space. The way that it has been designed with the return on the back wall encourages the focus to come back into the room, so the space as a whole does not feel like a corridor to another room. The colours and careful order keep the room feeling both livable and workable.

CENTREPIECE

A narrower width on the coffee table means it slots into the space perfectly. The fact that it's upholstered helps soften the space and there's no bruising of shins as you slide past to get into the sofa. It can also double as an extra seat.

Ways with mirrors

✳ You don't have to actually use an 'overmantle' mirror (one with a flat bottom edge and usually curved top); use any you like.

✳ Proportion counts. Ideally you want your mirror to be two-thirds the width of the mantelpiece. Then use this measurement to work out the ideal height of the mirror: proportionately a height of 1.5x the width works well for a rectangular mirror.

✳ Lean or hang? Leaning an overmantel mirror against the wall looks much less formal than hanging it. It's possible to secure it with chains to make sure it doesn't topple.

✳ The height you hang at matters too. Hanging a rectangular mirror within a whisker of the mantelpiece works best. A square needs a little more space (which depends on the proportions so I can't tell you exactly), and an oval or round mirror more still (30cm plus at least). All of these tips apply to artworks too.

The fireplace

In many living rooms the fireplace is the natural focal point, but it's also a key styling opportunity that's not to be missed. Use it as a platform for your personal style.

BALANCE AND SYMMETRY

Decide whether to work with or against symmetry. Working with symmetry could mean a row of several of the same type of item across the whole width or a pair of matching vases, one at either end. Working against it could mean a cluster of items, layering one in front of the other (see opposite, and below right), or it could mean using just a single 'high point' such as one vase and balancing it with cluster of items at the other side (see below). Play with what looks good – the trick is to stand back and look at your arrangement from a distance and keep changing it until you are happy with the result.

SCALE

Keep things in proportion. A large fireplace will need a large display on top to balance it, whilst a smaller one would look top heavy unless the display was scaled down.

THEME

Having a definite theme holds a display together. Theming with colour is one of the easiest ways to style, but you can also theme by type or texture (glass, ceramic or metal for example).

Dressing a hearth in summer

Once the weather gets warm and you stop lighting the fire, it can become a dead area in the room, but there are ways to style it so that it still feels full of life. Start by giving the whole hearth a good clean so that it doesn't look sooty.

✳ Lit church candles or votives en masse in the hearth will give off a similar warm glow that you're used to with a fire in the winter. Votives are inexpensive enough to use lavishly while church candles last for a long time so are good value.

✳ Place a vase of flowers or a potted plant (hydrangeas work well and flower for at least four weeks) in the hearth (not in it or it looks a bit naff, as if you're trying to hide something – you are!).

✳ Use a hide-it-all approach. Stand framed artworks, photos and posters in the hearth leaning against the fire surround. Then add a few smaller items in front – a vase or vases, a pile of books, a small object or two. The collection should end up looking as if it's meant to be there, rather than just hiding something.

✳ Go for the classic option and track down a fire screen that suits your scheme.

Creating 'tablescapes'

There are so many opportunities to create a series of vignettes in the living room – from the coffee table to the sideboard, any surface is game for a display. Just be confident in arranging your treasures in a way that reflects your personal style.

STYLING THE COFFEE TABLE

Just as the kitchen table is the hub of the kitchen, the coffee table is often the hub of the lounge. It's where your TV remote probably lives, teas and coffees are perched and newspapers piled. But it's also an opportunity to create another decorative feature in the room.

✳ Harden and level out the soft, squishy surfaces of upholstered coffee tables (ottomans, pouffes etc.) with a pile of large books or an oversized tray. I find a tray made from a waterproof material with deep sides extremely practical – it acts as a 'safety net' and stops any spills from drinks etc. from going everywhere.

✳ Soften things up with a throw – fold it to create a 'runner' that you can lay across the table. It will also hide a multitude of sins too (chocolate finger stains or spills), and it's another way to re-style the table when you fancy a different look.

✳ Use height to create interest. I group stacks of books and then use these as a platform for all my objects. But don't go too high – you want to be able to see over the top to the TV when you're lounging or make eye-contact with other people sat opposite you.

✳ Group smaller items in clusters so that your arrangement doesn't become too bitty – a platter, an open book or a small tray will all help to contain and order the items.

✳ Contain the clutter. A small open basket for the remotes will give them a 'home' that they're more likely to return to. Even the small gesture of putting folded papers in a pile on a large tray makes the place feel tidier.

✳ Don't fill the whole space. Leave room to put your feet up.

CONSOLES, SIDETABLES, SHELVES AND SIDEBOARDS

Any surface is game to a stylist – the same goes for you at home. Use them to showcase your beauties.

✳ Think about the viewpoint – a low surface such as a coffee table or side table will mostly be viewed from above – whereas a console table or sideboard will be viewed more side on. Place objects according to where they will be showcased best.

✳ Start with the largest key piece first. This might be a table lamp, or a vase or a painting. Then start to place things in relation to this.

✳ When placing objects consider how they look both one on top of the other and one in front of another. A series of different-sized bowls could be placed one inside the other or propped up against a wall, one in front of one another.

✳ Make use of your backdrop. An arrangement on a table that's positioned against a wall doesn't stop at the table; it can carry on and up the wall. Lean or hang frames, pictures and artwork to extend the display. Use the wall as your starting point and work forward from there, layering as you go.

✳ A piece of 'floating' furniture positioned away from a wall won't have a 'side' as such and will have to look good from all angles. As there's no wall to work from, use the centre of the table as your anchor (and highest point) and work out from there.

✳ Each time you refresh or create a new tablescape, always walk away from it so you can see it properly from all angles. The vignette should look good from any standpoint – just keep playing until you are happy with the results.

The finishing touches

A well-chosen sofa, a thoughtfully placed table, a nicely proportioned room. Even if you have all these elements in place, you may still feel that your living room does not have that magical 'finished' touch that you see in professionally styled rooms.

Stylists and designers use a variety of simple but highly effective elements to complete a room. Employ them yourself, and make them work to beautify and finish your space.

LIGHTING
This is key. It's simple; never use the ceiling fitting as the sole source of light in the room – this should be for decoration only. See it as the finishing touch, the jewel in the room. Instead, use a combination of task lighting; picture lights, floor lamps with directional heads for reading and mood lighting – low wattage table lamps or uplighters – positioning them where you need them.

SOFTEN THINGS UP
Comfort is everything in a lounge. Make yours look and feel inviting and comfortable by adding cushions and throws to chairs and sofas. These can be changed throughout the year – rotated when you fancy something new – or swapped according to season. Being able to reach out and pull over a throw whilst your watching a film without moving from your seat is a very good thing.

FRAGRANCE
Harness scent to alter the mood of the room. Fragrance that can be used in short bursts, such as a candle, a spray or an oil burner is ideal for the living room or any other room where you spend lots of time. Some fragrances can be too cloying if you're right up close to them for very long periods.

WINDOW TREATMENTS
Often the lounge is positioned at the front of the house which means privacy will be an issue. You may feel vulnerable even if you aren't overlooked, especially at night when you are looking out to pitch black but actually, it's more about preventing the sensation of being exposed, of feeling vulnerable. I like the feeling of being cocooned in a cosy space protected from the elements. It's amazing just how much heat is lost from an undressed window. Use curtains, blinds etc. as an opportunity to bring in the pattern, colour, texture and luxury you feel you need. (See page 249 for more ideas on curtains). Consider scale when choosing your curtains. Lined and interlined 'ballgown' style, voluminous curtains can become too

*Keep comfort at the forefront of your mind when adding the finishing touches. It's all about creating a space that appeals to the senses; fragrance to lift your spirits, light to create mood, rugs, throws and cushions to warm and flowers to add life and vitality.

intrusive and encroach on the space and light in a room. Unless you pull them right back to the sides of the window they could make a room lacking in natural light much darker.

RUGS
The right rug will ground and therefore finish a room because it will create the effect of holding everything else together. The choices are endless. There are deep pile rugs, flat weaves, large loop, small loop, silk, wool, cotton, woven, tufted and ragged rugs in each and every colour. The whole point of a rug is that it adds colour and pattern however subtle or bold. There are no hard and fast rules on the correct size for a rug, just your own opinions on what will look balanced and right in your space. You have to consider whether or not you like furniture to be positioned fully off the rug, or fully on the rug as this obviously will affect the rug size.

Kids' play zone

Give your children somewhere to play as this activity is one of the vital building blocks of their lives. It teaches them so many things, including how to be absorbed in their own worlds and imagination.

The idea of a dedicated playroom is supposed to mean that the rest of the house is not littered with children's toys. However, the reality is that most children under ten years old will always want to be in the same room as you. This means you have to take a flexible view and work out the best place to create a play zone that will work for you and your children.

FURNITURE
All children love to sit at their own table or desk, so make this a must-have in your playroom. Almost any piece of metal or wood furniture can be revived with a coat of paint so the desk does not have to be an expense. A small, comfortable sofa or a series of floor cushions is a good idea as well if there is room, as you will want to sit and read to and with them and it is far more likely to happen if you are both comfortable. Large beanbags are also a good option. Bring in items that inspire your child; a large acrylic mirror is great fun for everyone especially if you all like dressing up, acting and singing.

ZONE IT
Order the room by zone according to what will be happening in each area. An art zone might have an easel, a few shelves and lidded boxes for paints and papers; a bookcase, floor cushions, beanbag or sofa will set the scene for a reading corner. Because technology is so much a part of our lives, the child's table-desk will naturally morph into a computer area as they grow older and as you allow the room as a whole to adapt. All children appreciate having the middle of the room kept free for general play; a soft rug is a good idea because this is where a lot of activity will take place.

STORAGE
The play zone is going to get messy – the trick is to design the space so that it is easy-ish to tidy up quickly and the best way of doing that is to have storage in all its forms where possible. Some furniture can double as both furniture and storage – trunks and other lidded boxes are very useful especially if they are on wheels, as you can move them in and out of use as and when needed. Plastic buckets are good for smaller toy storage and can be labelled to encourage some order. Open shelves or alcove-style shelving are excellent solutions for keeping the playroom tidy and organised. There will always be some toys that you cannot stow away, short of creating an entire wall of hidden storage behind sliding doors, but they can be housed on a sideboard or at one end of a long table (see above right).

Creating a play zone
If space is an issue, it's possible to create a play zone within another room. Built-in, floor-to-ceiling cupboards with plenty of space for toys would work well in conjunction with two or three boxes that can be wheeled in and out of the cupboard when needed. Boxes on castors also work for storage beneath a table or desk (see above). The key to making a play zone work in a multi-functional space is to work with the scheme that surrounds it. When the toy zone is in action, there will be plenty of colour and amusement for all, but, when everything is put away, you gain back that sense of adult space because you have kept the room as a whole consistent in its design.

THE DEN
Once children hit the age of 11 or 12, they much prefer a den as they want somewhere to be with their friends. In a large house you may want to create a separate kids' living room (see opposite, far right). Beanbags and pouffes really come into their own in a scheme like this. A good audio visual system would also be a great, if luxurious feature in a den.

*The success of a play zone will depend on how easily you (or your children) can tidy it up. Where practical, use every available inch of wall space for shelving or alcoves (see left) or fit shelves into alcoves and voids within the architecture (see below left) to maximise on potential storage points. Movable toy boxes (see below right) make the most of a space as they can also double as side tables.

*This is a gift of a space for any young person as it has been dedicated to the freedom to create (and make a mess too). It has the perfect balance of order and fun – the simple box shelving gives more than enough space for storing the art kit neatly, but the genius of the space is the large blackboard wall (see page 203 for how to do this), as this makes the room feel totally liberated from normal living constraints. The small desks and colourful stools add the final touch and are also practical.

KITCHENS and DINING

It usually happens that as we mature, literally and emotionally, our homes take on greater importance to us. Then within our homes, the kitchen emerges as one of most valued spaces of all, taking on a meaningful aspect that goes far beyond function.

We learn to cook, to entertain, to nurture. We become the next generation of hosts, as families change and grow. As our lives alter and become busier, our kitchen and dining areas have to work harder for us. They are far more to us than places to cook in, consume in and clean. Kitchens can be challenging, potentially awkward spaces, varying in size from the smallest of galleys to the generously proportioned. For some, kitchen and dining spaces are one. For others, the main dining table is in another room entirely. Whatever layout and space you have to work with, there are ways and tricks to shape your kitchen and dining space to make it not only useful and practical, but characterful and pleasing too.

The kitchen – the heart of the home?

The kitchen belongs to everyone; the person that cooks, the child that plays, the neighbour that calls. The celebrations that happen, the friends who arrive, the first morning tea and the evening's last beer; all meet together in this central, nurturing room.

THE KITCHEN AS EMOTIONAL LINCHPIN

Amidst the pots and pans, tins, packets and stowed-away mops, it is easy to forget the emotional importance of the kitchen in a home. It is here that the kettle is endlessly boiled, to greet a friend or to comfort those in distress. The fridge door is opened and shut and wine is poured in celebration, commiseration and seduction. Noticeboards heave with reminders, and chalkboards and calendars are scribbled on. Flour is sifted and sugar is measured nervously for that pride-filled first birthday cake. Late nights leave candles burnt to the wick.

The kitchen has a life of its very own, and is witness to all the ups and downs of everyday life. The kitchen table, as the focus, is one of our most trusty, utilised, taken-for-granted pieces of furniture. A place for homework, Play-Doh, crafts, letter writing, bill sorting, daydreaming and every meal from breakfast to the tipsy midnight feast. It may not be the most expensive item we ever buy, but it is usually the one we rely on, use the most and keep for the longest.

A true working kitchen which is used and loved will rarely be spotless or totally organised, and neither should it be. Like those that people it, it is not flawless or static, but is a room that is always busy, waiting to play host to the next meal or moment. The most beautiful kitchens are those that are enjoyed, played in and worked in as the true, living and vibrant core of the home.

The table

Without doubt, the table is the centrepiece of a kitchen. But it's far more than just a table. It's the action zone for nearly everything from homework to food preparation to actual dining. This is where you'll hear stories, tell stories, eat, love, argue, cry and put the world to rights.

The multi-functional kitchen

Kitchens are so much more than spaces to prepare food: much of family life takes place there. Often referred to as 'the heart of the home', the kitchen has become just this, the chief communal room hosting the playroom, dining zone, home office and more.

FIVE TIPS FOR MAKING A MULTI-FUNCTIONAL KITCHEN WORK

1 Start by getting the flow (how you move round the room) and the mix (the balance between functionality and comfort) right. Define the room's various functions by zoning it into cooking, eating, working, playing and chilling. As you work up your ideas, always remember that this is where you and your family will be spending the majority of their home time, so it must feel comfortable to all the senses. What the room looks like and how you respond to it is key.

2 Beware noisy appliances like washing machines and dryers – before buying, check their noise ratings. There's nothing worse than a din interrupting your den-time, down-time or dinner-time.

3 If you are going to be using the kitchen as a snug, an informal TV room or a playroom during the day, furnish it as you would those other rooms. Just because it's the kitchen doesn't mean the furniture has to be kitchen-esque. See it as another opportunity to flaunt your style, bringing in decorative elements to soften its functional kitcheny aspects. So, while lighting needs to be functional, you may be able to add a gorgeous chandelier or sculptural floor lamp. Whatever your taste, functionality must come first, though with your choice of upholstery for sofas and chairs. A loose cover that can be whipped off and cleaned relatively easily is far more practical than fixed upholstery. Alternatively, have your new upholstery professionally treated to avoid the horrible upset of marks and stains.

4 Multi-functional kitchens are at work almost round the clock, so it is important to consider the transition between day and night. One way of doing so is through lighting. It has become the norm in other rooms of the house to control the lighting by having different circuits or dimmers. Being able to create a soft, warm light for dining is as important as having enough light for the children to do their homework or for you to cook.

5 Storage is key to making multi-functional rooms work; you have to be able to put things back in their place, ready for the next 'shift' in the kitchen. Toys away in their boxes, art and school homework hidden behind cupboard doors, wipe-clean tablecloths stashed in a drawer – these are basics. Then style your way through making the room work for adults – set out different china, dim the lights and light some candles.

7 ways to give a kitchen a sense of space

Kitchens are easily overwhelmed by not only the larger pieces they house, but by the utensils, gadgets, cookery books and stuff of life that gathers here.

1 Make use of the wall space and hanging space. A wall-mounted pan rack or rail or a ceiling-hung batterie de cuisine both look good and will save valuable space in cupboards and drawers. If they're positioned near the cooking space, they'll get coated in a film of grease (sounds grim, but it's true), but it's no big deal to put them in the dishwasher every couple of months. And since you'll be using the pans themselves all the time, they won't have time to get dirty.

2 The insides of cupboard doors and the back of the kitchen door provide useable space for all sorts of things – pan lids on a rack, shopping bags, aprons, spice racks and more.

3 If you have to fit a dining area into a small space, opt for adaptable furniture – an extending table with stools or benches that can slip right underneath works well. And remember, they do not all have to match. Mixing is good (see page 210 for more ideas).

4 Keep the surfaces as clutter-free as you can. It makes a huge difference to the perception of space.

5 A lighter space looks bigger. Paint walls a light colour, allow as much daylight in as you can, add more lights or, if possible, up the wattage in existing ones. You could even go as far as using mirrored or highly reflective glass or metal splashbacks.

6 Ditch the wall-hung head-height cabinets in favour of open shelving – it will give you just as much storage space, but won't feel as oppressive as cupboards. You'll also have the advantage of being able to customise the depth of the shelves. If cupboards are your thing though, go for half-depth cupboards that encroach less into the space.

7 If you're really running out of space, have a 'satellite' piece of furniture in another part of the house to act as an overflow. A cupboard, chest or cabinet, can all be re-purposed to store things you perhaps don't need so often.

Getting organised

The trick to having a kitchen that functions properly, without clutter or stress, is order and organisation. Arrange your storage in a way that works well for you.

THE BIG DE-CLUTTER

Make an inventory of your kitchen kit – the waffle maker, the pineapple slicer, the electric carving knife, the baking kit, plates and glasses – everything. Get rid of things you don't use. Be brutal.

RANK BY USE

Organise what you're left with into everyday, regularly used and seldom-used items. You want the everyday items in easily reached places and seldom-used things kept higher up or at the backs of cupboards. Move things that only come out once or twice a year, or are very season-led, to another part of the house. Giant-size turkey platters, picnicware, thermos flasks, and preserving pans can all live in the garage or attic until they're needed.

CUSTOMISE

Customise the space inside drawers and cupboards. Use drawer tidies or small baskets to divide large drawers, and larger baskets or extra shelves in cupboards spaced exactly to suit a set of glasses or a row of storage jars.

STORE, PREP, COOK, EAT, CLEAN

Think of the key functions and where they take place. Position the items needed for each as close as you can to that area. Spices near the cooker, plates near the dishwasher and sink, tea and coffee, cups and teapots near the kettle.

LESS IS MORE

The less you have on display, the bigger the kitchen will look. Unless something is a thing of beauty or is used a few times a week, store it out of sight. I like to keep some things handy for cooking and cleaning though; a collection of cooking oils (the ones I use daily, not all of them), plus salt and pepper by the cooker, and some basic cleaning items by the sink.

THE PROJECT:

A chalkboard

The kitchen often acts a family organisational hub. Go one step beyond having a calendar pinned to the wall to keep the family on track and instead have a chalkboard wall for making notes, writing shopping lists and highlighting diary dates. Use blackboard paint to paint the area you want. Your chalkboard will look much more impressive when it's wall-to-wall and floor-to-ceiling.

HOW TO:

✳ First, prepare the surface. If it's already painted with matt emulsion, you need do no more than apply the blackboard paint with a brush or roller. If you're painting on top of vinyl paint, wood or metal, you'll need to prepare the surface first with a couple of coats of the appropriate primer.

✳ Apply at least three coats for the best possible finish, allowing them to dry between coats.

✳ This paint can be quite gloopy, make sure you mix it thoroughly before using – otherwise you'll be left with a thick unworkable paint when you come to the bottom of the tin.

*Keep everyday cooking essentials handy by the cooker. Using a large tile, a tray, a platter or a chopping board means there's a home for them to go back to and it'll stay looking tidy.

Display versus storage

You'll know whether you're the kind of person who likes things on display or prefers to keep things well hidden. A carefully curated and edited display can be as beautiful as it is functional.

*Open storage is both a practical and stylish solution in the kitchen. Replacing wall-hung units with rows of shelving keeps the everyday close to hand (see above), whilst a small wall-hung unit (see above right) and a traditional dresser (see right) showcase pretty crockery.

What works

✳ Don't let your open shelves become a random hotchpotch; be disciplined in choosing what goes where and don't allow clutter to creep in. You're after 'carefully curated' not chaos.

✳ Patterned and colourful crockery looks great pretty much any way you choose to display it, but it's useful for breaking up swathes of the more basic everyday items – such as clear glasses and plain white dinnerware. Spread these basics out into multiple small blocks rather than long rows of the same thing.

✳ Make even the basics as good-looking as possible. If you've got dry foodstuffs out on display, invest in a matching set of stylish tins or jars to decant them into.

✳ Pan-racks suspended from the ceiling are real space savers (see page 200), but they also create a strong kitchen display, especially if you have a beautiful set of steel or copper pans.

✳ Always provide yourself with some closed storage – there's always something that you'll want to hide.

Styling the kitchen

Bring all the same decorative touches to the kitchen as you would to any other room in the house. Wallpaper, artworks, books, flowers and of course, photos of you and the children and their masterpieces all have a place in the kitchen.

*Think outside the box when it comes to storing certain groceries. Fruit and vegetables make instant, gorgeous displays when stored in cake stands (see left) or piled into clear vases, and a bunch of herbs can look just as gorgeous as a bunch of flowers (see bottom left).

*Bring energy and personality to the room with colourful cards and photos (see opposite). In dry areas away from the sink and hob it's perfectly okay to use wallpaper (see above). An oilcloth for the table is as practical as it is pretty (see left).

Piecing together the dining room

The main table and seating arrangement, like a bed or a sofa, is central to our lives and needs, and for this reason, comfort, function, ease of use and general good looks, must all work together.

The table

THE FEEL

A kitchen table or dining table is a big ticket buy. It is also the largest piece in the room and greatly influences the look and feel of the space. It's easy to be blinded by too much choice – start to narrow down your options by working out the 'feel' you're after. Traditional or modern? Ultra-polished chic or laid-back rustic?

THE COMFORT FACTOR

Comfort needs to be considered too. Do the legs of the table you are thinking of buying get in the way of legs or knees? Is it a good height to comfortably fit long legs?

WHAT'S IT MADE OF?

Also, think about the material; wood feels warm and welcoming to the touch; glass and marble feel much colder. Have you considered how to care for your table-top? You don't want to be constantly worrying about the table's upkeep, so check the maintenance requirements if you're buying a new piece. Will you want to be able to prepare food freely on the surface without the worry of stains and marks? Would the children be free to let loose with their homework and artworks? If you're going for wood, an oiled or varnished surface is tougher than one that's polished or waxed.

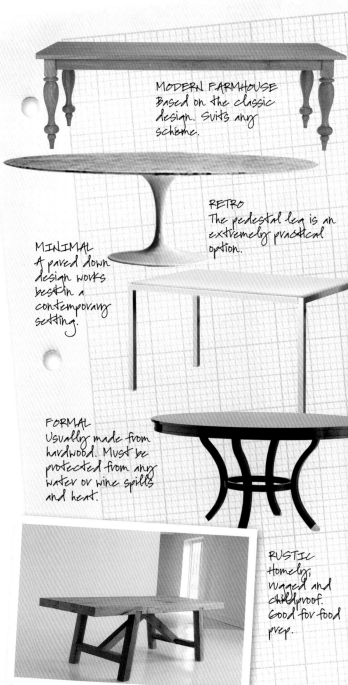

MODERN FARMHOUSE
Based on the classic design. Suits any scheme.

RETRO
The pedestal leg is an extremely practical option.

MINIMAL
A pared down design works best in a contemporary setting.

FORMAL
Usually made from hardwood. Must be protected from any water or wine spills and heat.

RUSTIC
Homely, waxed and childproof. Good for food prep.

How to work out the size of the table you need

* When choosing the table, think about how many it must seat on a daily basis and how many more you need to add and how often for parties, high days and holidays.

* As a general rule, allow 70cm of table space per person. Bear in mind that you'll be able to fit more people round an oval or circular table than round a square or rectangular one – and ovals and circles are more sociable as your guests will all be able to see and hear one another.

* To work out the size of table that will fit your space, allow at least 1m between table and wall or other furniture for the chair to be pulled out. If you are short of space, have you got room for an extending table? This will give you the greatest flexibility.

BENCHES

A pair of benches is a practical option in a small space as they can be pushed beneath the table. They are also very handy when you need to squeeze a few more people around the table as everyone can all shuffle up a little. Use an upholstered bench cushion to soften it, or add individual cushions to demarcate everyone's seat.

STOOLS ETC.

Stools, cubes and pouffes are fantastically flexible and are a great stand by to have in the house. I have several that act as bedside tables, occasional tables or display plinths for artwork, books or flowers. I pull them in to use at the table as and when I need to. I would advise topping them with a comfortable cushion if you're using them regularly for seating.

BENCH
A great space saver offering the most flexibility.

ARMCHAIR STYLE
offers the most comfort, but also takes up more space.

UPHOLSTERED
A comfortable take on a classic chair – roomy without being too bulky.

UPHOLSTERED BENCH
Comfort and flexibility in one. An ultra glam look which suits a sitting room.

STACKABLE
Ideal for using as extra emergency chairs as they store easily.

Small spaces

✳ Going bespoke maximises even the tightest of spaces – like a window sill, above. At a push it (cosily) seats four diners.
✳ Pushing a table against the wall when not in use will save you about 1m of floor space.
✳ Choose clear acrylic, light-coloured, delicate-looking furniture over dark 'blocky' pieces as they encroach on the space less. Shiny metallic finishes have the same effect.

The seating

CHAIRS

The classic arrangement is to use a pair of carvers (chairs with arms) at either end of the table with armless chairs running down each side. Style matters of course, but comfort is an important consideration if you're intending to be chatting at the table for hours after dinner. Individual chairs with upholstered seats are probably the most popular choice, with upholstered 'armchair' styles being the most comfortable but the most space-hungry.

For some of us, the height of the back of the chair matters as much as the width in terms of comfort, however chairs with low backs that can slip beneath the table are fantastic space savers.

*To match or not to match? Your table and chairs do not have to match – nor do your chairs have to be a matching set. In my flat in London, I've mixed a white French upholstered sofa with a wooden bench on the opposite side and two stackable wooden backed chairs at either end. I love the flexibility that the mix gives me.

A dining sofa

For the ultimate in comfort opt for an upholstered bench seat or sofa as either will create the feel of a 'dining salon'. For such a piece to work, the seat height needs to be roughly 45cm high. A sofa or bench with be easier to access if the arms are low.

Dining in an open-plan space

Kitchen living has become so central to our lives that few of us still have dedicated dining rooms, choosing instead to make a dining zone within an open-plan kitchen. Pay attention to the lighting so that you can set the mood appropriately, give the area its own identity through colour or choice of materials and, where possible, try to make the arrangement flexible so you can maximise on its daily use.

MADE TO MEASURE FIXED SEATING

Built-in seats or banquettes maximises the available space and helps to squeeze the largest number of seats around a table. Lift-up seats mean they double as extra storage. Designing them to face out in an L-shape towards the rest of the room like this, means that you create the right 'flow' and 'focal points' in the room. The kickboard beneath the bench matches the floor and the base of the kitchen units, which makes the banquette appear to 'float'. It also adds to the seamless look.

MOVEABLE FURNITURE

Chunky castors with wheel locks allow the table to move for easy access to the banquette. Away from meal times, the table can be pushed back into the corner. The stools live under the table when not in use and can be pushed together to form a bench, when extra seats are needed.

THE LIGHTING

Using totally non-kitcheny-style lighting like these patterned shades softens the dining space and gives it a decorative feel rather than being purely functional.

THE FRAMES ON THE WALL

The dining area is given its own identity with black-and-white framed prints. This simple decorative element helps 'zone' the corner so that it reads as 'dining' rather than 'kitchen'. The shots of yellow – the cushions and the stools – reinforce this.

How to light the dining table

Lighting should be atmospheric and flattering. Dimmers and candlelight are crucial to create a warm, inviting atmosphere. A statement light will add drama and elegance to the room. Any pendant lamp should be centralised over the table – you may need to extend out from the fitting with chain or flex if it's off-centre. Allow clearance of at least 70cm below. Play with scale; a supersized floor lamp (below) or a cluster of small pendants are witty modern alternatives to a chandelier.

8 ways to make your table elegant

There are unavoidable moments in life when meals are rushed. Food on the run is invariably forgettable and unenjoyable. Preparing food at home allows it to be savoured as it should be; with a little less haste and a lot more style. A single morning coffee or the humblest of snacks can be elevated by pretty china, decent cutlery and a few additional touches.

1 Try to position your table to take advantage of any windows or doors. In spring and summer it's a joy to be able to throw them open to let the fresh air in and the view can be admired all year.

2 Candles make any mealtime feel special. I light a candle pretty much every dinner time, even for mid-week suppers. It's become a ritual of mine that's as ingrained now as putting out the cutlery.

3 Be thoughtful. Carefully consider everything you put on the table, from the salt and pepper pots or grinders to the water jug, napkins and placemats. It's the small details that set the scene and make the food taste better.

4 Don't save the best for guests or special occasions, instead use it and enjoy it everyday. Put out linen napkins even when it's just the family. The same goes for pretty china and glassware.

5 'Upgrade' condiments by decanting them into pretty containers. Small bowls are perfect for salt and pepper and mustards (serve with a mini teaspoon). Use chunky generous pots for store-bought chutneys and jams or better still, make your own from scratch so that you can control right from the start what they are packaged in.

6 Use a flat plate, small tray, platter or tile as a 'frame' that brings together condiments – salt, pepper, mustards, soy sauce – whatever it is that you need for that meal. This is a technique I use again and again at home in various rooms. It's a way to tidy up a cluster of items so they become a unified collection.

7 Invest in some beautiful everyday luxuries. These will be different for each family, depending on what you love to eat and your routine. In our house, it's the following that make the difference to our day-to-day: a beautiful olive-wood cutting board that's used to serve up everything from breads, pizza and cheese to antipasti and salad; a top-quality, beautifully designed, solid-feeling pepper grinder; beeswax candles and linen napkins.

8 Add flowers. Even just a few stems of something chopped from the garden and popped into a jam jar makes all the difference.

Piecing together your 'set'

For most of us, the days of buying a whole matching formal dinner set for 'best' have gone. The way we live and entertain has changed; many people now prefer to entertain at the kitchen table rather than in a formal dining room setting.

Lack of space too often means that there just isn't cupboard space for two dinner sets. But when you no longer have those formal guidelines, it can be difficult to decide how to piece together a collection that is tailored to your needs on a practical level, but that also looks the part.

FROM A PRACTICAL POINT OF VIEW
* How many pieces to buy? That not only depends on how many you are, but on how often you entertain and the food you serve. I tend to buy in tens and twelves. It's especially useful to have enough side plates to cover starters and desserts when you're entertaining. That way there's no need to do a rushed wash in between courses.
* What pieces work best? This means thinking about the food you like to eat. There's no point buying shallow soup bowls if you regularly serve up meal-in-a-bowl Japanese broths.
* How can I make the most of what I buy? In this case, versatility is good. Seek out items that will be multi-functional by looking beyond their specified use. A well-designed bowl can swing between soups, pasta dishes and sweets. Serve up chocolate mousse in espresso cups. If you're stumped for ideas, see how food has been styled for books and magazines.
* If you eat outside a lot during the summer months, think about buying a more robust set that is more practical for outdoor dining.

FROM A STYLE POINT OF VIEW
* Think of your tableware as a collection of related but not too 'matchy-matchy' pieces that you can put together for a 'layered' personal effect.
* Be as creative in making your choices as you would be picking the accessories for any room in the house. What you choose should reflect your signature style.
* Instead of buying one matching dinner service, treat each element of a place setting as a matching set. So, for example, buy dinner plates that all match each other, plus soup bowls that all match each other, and so on. Then play with layering these pieces to create different looks or 'outfits' for each meal. Use plain china to offset busy patterns.
* Don't forget that cutlery, table linen and glassware are other sorts of layers that add to the effect. Think about how all these layers will work together when you're out shopping.

The art of dressing up a table

When you're having friends over for dinner it's always nice to raise the bar and make a special effort with the table.

THE FEEL

＊ Think about this as being theatre. Who is your 'audience'? The girls for tea (delicate ribbon-tied napkins, floral china and a jug of blousy flowers), or are you serving up hearty bowls of chilli at half time for those emotionally embroiled in the rugby (paper napkins, chunky bowls, spoons and a cloth-free table)? Plan the feeling; romantic, fun, decadent, and then style to suit. Remember that the food and the people around the table are the lead characters.

＊ Be appropriate, if you are introducing your fiancé to family members you will feel more comfortable if you take a conventional approach (matching dinner plates, best glasses, really good flowers and proper napkins). However, if it's you and very close friends be as surprising and as eccentric as you want to be as they will love that (an extraordinary amount of candles, a totally different placesetting for each person and tea towels in place of napkins).

THE ESSENTIALS

＊ You should always have one good set of white china (stoneware, earthenware or porcelain). Use this as your base on which to layer all the other coloured or patterned elements as and when you want to; the hotchpotch of patterned side plates picked up at a car boot, or a set of bowls inherited from your granny.

＊ In order for the mis-matching to work, you need to have a significant number of things matching or it will start to look bitty.

＊ Make sure things are easy to access; have more that one water jug and multiple condiments so all guests can reach them. I place salt and pepper and any sauces etc. together on a small plate or tray to make a condiment 'hub' and then place a few of these down the length of the table – having them on a plate also makes it easier to pass along.

THE ATMOSPHERE

＊ Candles are an absolute must for the table at night. I light a candle pretty much every mealtime – even during the week or when it's just the two of us.

＊ Don't use scented candles, as their strong fragrance will interfere with the food. Beeswax candles are fine though, as their honeyed scent is gentle.

＊ To give sufficient light to eat by, use a candelabra or a few candlesticks; dinner candles give off much more light that votives. I like to place votives on either a mirror or a series of mirror tiles – it doubles the light and the twinkle (see right).

THE LITTLE EXTRAS

＊ There are plenty of opportunities to add layers of decoration from the simple to the extravagant. Think about the small details – everything is seen up close. Napkins are a good device to use – an

ornate napkin ring acts as jewellery for the table – or you could just use a length of ribbon, securing a flower stem in place as an extra decoration before placing a name card on top (see below right).

✳ A vase of something – if you'll be sitting at the table for dinner keep arrangements low (30cm maximum). Keep the flowers appropriate in style too; informal and loose for a mid-week dinner, more showy for a special occasion. Steer clear of powerfully scented blooms – you don't want any fragrance to interfere with your delicious food.

Tablecloths

✳ Generally speaking you want an overhang of at least 25cm on all sides or the tablecloth will look mean.

✳ They don't actually have to be tablecloths – I often buy cotton and linen by the length to use as a tablecloth. Most fabrics are 150cm wide, which, for an average table (roughly 80cm wide) will give enough overhang to look and feel comfortable. Sometimes I hem the raw edges, but sometimes I just fray them.

✳ Patterned cloths can be beautiful and are a great way to dress the table if your china is relatively plain. I tend to hunt out fabrics I love rather than buy 'proper' patterned tablecloths.

✳ Oil cloth: a practical option as it's wipeable. It is great for outside, or for inside when you're painting, baking or doing craft projects at the kitchen table. They are available in many gorgeous colours and patterns.

✳ Heat protector: use under a tablecloth to protect a fine table such as one with a French-polished top.

✳ A runner: this is normally about 40cm wide, but it's best to be guided by the proportions of your table. It looks good with an overhang of around 15cm, or when it just kisses the floor. Or use two runners down each side of the table as an alternative to placemats.

Styling the table for a party

Playing the host is one of life's greatest pleasures. Be it tea for two on a weekday afternoon, or a sit down dinner for ten for a special birthday, creating the table scene is all part of the fun.

*Have some fun with the details and find unusual ways of presenting things. A series of cloches covering a selection of chocolates on a marble chopping board makes a great dessert centrepiece (see above). Expresso cups are the perfect size for mini biscuits and bells tied to a bottle let guests know the bubbles are heading their way.

✳ Make life easy for yourself and lay out the table with all the things guests need so that they can help themselves. All the essentials should be within easy reach (napkins, plates, cutlery etc.). Bottle openers always seem to disappear, so buy an extra one and tie it to something so it's got a home for the night (the ice bucket holding the beers or white wine is ideal).

✳ Zone the table, grouping smaller items together (glasses for example) and positioning the largest item (here, the foliage centrepiece) in the middle. Arrange the rest of the things by working outwards from the centre, placing small items in rows and columns. Imagine there's a grid running over the table to keep you on track. That way things don't look as if they've just been flung on the table.

✳ I've built up an arsenal of servingware over the years, collecting patterned and plain, old and new as and when I've come across something. It's a pleasure to have a choice rather than panicking at the last minute about whether you have enough. The same goes for cutlery. For buffets, I've been buying silver-plate cutlery whenever I come across it really cheap at car boot sales or on eBay. With a little TLC you'll find that they come back to life and are perfect to use for parties, where it doesn't matter that you haven't got a full matching set. The same goes for plates – with enough mis-matching, it will look right.

✳ Play with the scale of the portioning. One generously proportioned dessert or a platter of pretty bite-sized treats is much more impressive than two or three average-sized portions. Think one large decorative bowl or twenty cute expresso cups filled with chocolate mousse.

✳ For covering a party table, use an especially large tablecloth that falls nearly to the floor on all sides. A tablecloth with a skimpy overhang just looks mean. If you don't have a suitably generous cloth, you can improvise by using a simple white bed sheet or by layering multiple tablecloths one on top of the other.

*Floral displays at parties need to be on a large scale – something short and squat will just get lost in the crowd. On a budget? Go for a large foliage-only display and then dot a few smaller vases of flowers by the food and drink – where you know they won't be missed.

Dressing your table with a bow

It's super cute and super easy. You'll need some pins and two lengths of wide ribbon: one long enough to go around the table, the other approximately 140cm for the bow. Start at the middle of the back edge with one end of it, pinning the ribbon to the tablecloth as you work your way around the table. Then finish with a big bow.

the HOME OFFICE

The joy of working from home is that there aren't any corporate rules stating what your work space should look like and there's nobody to insist you use this chair or that desk. You only have to suit yourself. Your requirements will be personal and unique, so consider them carefully, whether you're a fully fledged full-time homeworker or simply need somewhere to tackle the household admin in an organised fashion.

Technology has completely revolutionised how we work and more and more people are taking advantage of working on the hoof, not only from different locations in their homes, but from their local café, sometimes from the car and, when necessary, from their friends' homes. It all depends on your lifestyle and how you like to work. I work just as often from bed with the laptop perched on my knees as I do at the kitchen table. I like the immediacy and lack of formality. Working this way just doesn't feel like work.

Piecing the home office together

First of all, don't think you have to buy office furniture just because it's going in your office. This is especially critical if your office has to double as a spare room or is in the corner of the kitchen/diner or living room.

THE DESK
A desk doesn't have to be a 'desk'. It can be any shape, size or style. In a small space, a console table or a floating shelf hung at desk height could work a treat. A good average working height is around 73cm from the floor. Next, consider how big an area of desk you need. Give yourself room to spread out if your work dictates, but it's possible to make do with a surprisingly small amount of space, as long as you've got a good storage and filing system. And think about the material of your desktop. Glass and metal are cold to the touch but wood and leather are warming.

THE CHAIR
Multi-adjustable corporate office chairs are designed to accommodate literally any body. You only need to find a single chair that fits yours. Hunt down one that's comfortable and looks good too, in any style and of any type that appeals to you. If you move around in the office quite a bit as you work – reaching to the printer to collect pages or to access files or books – consider a chair with castors but bear in mind that castors will be a hindrance rather than a help if your flooring is a thick pile carpet.

THE TECHNOLOGY
If your work is computer-based, plan your layout to accommodate the technology. Getting the computer, printer, scanner and copier in the right places will create the best workflow as well as minimising the spaghetti-wire effect. The right layout is different for everyone, so take time to work out what's best for you and your working day.

THE OTHER FURNITURE
If space allows, bring in non-officey furniture for extra storage or to create a relaxed area for reading. It's a real treat to be able to sit in a wing chair to read, for example, rather than religiously having to sit bolt upright at the desk. Side tables, benches or cubes will all provide an attractive place for the overflow of piles of books or papers, and could also house a printer or stationery.

THE LIGHTING
Adequate lighting is a must. A desk lamp that's adjustable in height and direction is the best option, though the right table lamp could work too.

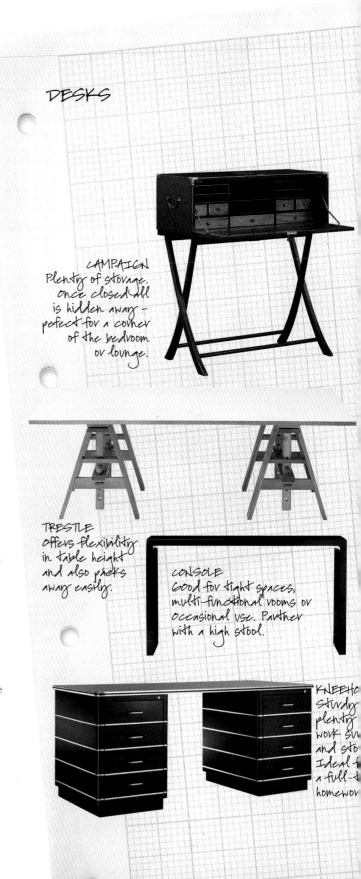

DESKS

CAMPAIGN
Plenty of storage. Once closed all is hidden away – pefect for a corner of the bedroom or lounge.

TRESTLE
offers flexibility in table height and also packs away easily.

CONSOLE
Good for tight spaces, multi-functional rooms or occasional use. Partner with a high stool.

KNEEHO
Sturdy
plenty
work su
and sto
Ideal f
a full-t
homewor

*To avoid the corporate office look, steer clear of office supply shops and head to home stores instead. Design and style your office in the way you would the rest of the house. In this office, silk 'ballgown' curtains, decorative accessories, a beautiful desk and clever shelving make it feel anything but officey.

Getting the feel just right

Many of us don't have the luxury of choosing which room to allocate as a home office. In an ideal world, it would have plenty of natural light, an inspiring view to gaze upon and would be situated in a quiet part of the house away from all distractions.

Wherever you have your work space, there are ways to create a comfortable room that's a pleasure to use – one where you'll feel good even if you're working.

PLAN THE LAYOUT
Spend time working out the best layout, coming at it from a functional point of view first (where is the power socket for the computer?) but also taking into account how the layout might change the feel of the room. I don't know the first thing about Feng Shui, but I do know that it just doesn't feel right to sit at a desk with

*I'll often cut a tiny arrangement for my desk with scented foliage such as lemon balm that releases its fragrance when touched.

Fragrancing an office
Fresh, uplifting, reviving scents are best in the office. This is not where you want to be relaxing. I use essential oils in a burner (well away from my paperwork). Green aromas such as basil, thyme, coriander and rosemary are all said to have a stimulating effect on brain. As do citrus-based fragrances such as grapefruit and lemon balm. (See page 134 for more ideas on fragrance).

your back to the door. It's much nicer to be facing the door or to be side on to it. Try it for yourself and you'll see what I mean. Most people need two main work areas: one in front of the computer and then another space for paperwork and phone calls.

POSITION THE DESK
Don't think you have to anchor your desk to a wall. If your desk has a good back view, try positioning it away from the walls, perhaps even right in the middle of the room. Just remember you'll need about 1m clearance from the desk to the wall behind your chair for comfortable access.

THINK ABOUT WINDOWS
Consider the location of the windows. Avoid eye strain caused by glare on your computer screen by not positioning the computer with the screen facing a window. And if you're one of those people who's easily distracted, don't put the desk in front of a window where something's likely to catch your eye.

PROVIDE WARMTH AND AIR
A comfortable working temperature is around 21°C, but if you have to sit still for long periods of time, you may need to increase that by a couple of degrees. And don't forget to open windows regularly. Stale air and a stuffy room don't promote clear thinking.

MAKE IT PERSONAL
If you dread the work you have to do in your home office, don't make it worse by making the area miserable. Choose the décor with as much consideration as you would another room. Colour and pattern have their place here, as do decorative objects. Bring in artworks, mirrors, plants or vases of flowers to personalise the space and make it a room you want to go to.

DISGUISE IT
There are ways to disguise office furniture and accessories if you've already invested in it. Using colour and pattern is the simplest. Wallpaper a boring steel filing cabinet or paint it a bold glossy colour; re-cover the seat of a standard office chair in a fabric you love or cover box files with colourful wrapping paper. (See pages 110–111 for more tips on overhauling what you've already got.)

When you don't have a room

Not everyone has the space to dedicate a whole room to a home office, but if you're in desperate need of somewhere to work, there are plenty of options. It's possible to carve out a desk area in the most unassuming or surprising of places.

CHOOSING YOUR SPOT

You may not have many location possibilities but if you do, consider how much peace and quiet you'll get. Is that spot in a main thoroughfare? Will the children constantly want your attention? If the spot is in an open-plan room, think about what else will be going on at the same time as you're intending to work. Watching TV, listening to music or to the children practice the violin aren't conducive to concentration or quiet phone calls. Other considerations are finding a space that has good natural light levels and easy access to power sockets.

BUILDING IN A DESK

Commission a carpenter to build a mini-office to fit the space you have. This could either be in a wall-to-wall bank of cupboards behind closed doors, which will also give you additional storage, located in an alcove, in an under stairs area or in some other overlooked spot. These are the basic considerations to bear in mind:

✳ In a shallow space such as an alcove, you'll probably need to fit a pull-out desk surface on runners to extend the available work space and allow for a more comfortable working position with enough room for your legs. The best way to do this is to fit one fixed shelf across the alcove, with another underneath on runners (see right). The fixed shelf is the ideal place for a desk lamp or a computer screen, whilst the bottom moveable shelf is perfect for a keyboard and paperwork. Allow a few centimetres clearance if you can between the shelves, so that you don't have to clear your desk after working each time.

✳ A comfortable desk height is 70–76cm, so aim for this.

✳ Install extra power sockets right by the desk if you can. You could trail an extension lead neatly from the nearest power point, but it will just make your desk look like an afterthought.

✳ If it's built into a cupboard, don't make the doors too wide if you're short on space – you'll have to keep a large area in front of the cupboard free to give you room to open them. Two narrow doors might work better than one big one. If space is really tight go for a sliding door.

✳ The doors need to open 180 degrees so they can swing right back nearly flush with the cupboard. Standard 90-degree hinges will make you feel hemmed in and claustrophobic.

✳ Use the space on the inside of the doors for additional storage. Hooks and shallow wire racks come in handy for holding various bits and bobs. Position these carefully, so that they work when the cupboard doors are shut.

*Now you see it, now you don't. A pull-down work area within an open-plan kitchen/diner is held securely in place when in use, with super strong chains. It was cleverly designed to match in with the kitchen units once closed.

Adapting an existing piece of furniture to make a desk area

It's surprisingly easy to adapt a wardrobe, chest or cabinet to accommodate a desk area. First strip out any rails and re-position or remove shelves that are in the wrong place. Then fit a pull-out work surface at the correct height (see left). You could even go as far as wallpapering or painting the interior to make it extra special.

Working in a multi-functional space

Kitchens, bedrooms and guest rooms can all be brought into use as a home office without restricting their original function. Here's how.

DECIDE WHICH FUNCTION WINS

Does your room function first as an office space and then as a spare bedroom second? Or vice versa? With careful planning and some compromise it's possible to accommodate both functions, but there will always be something that may have to be sacrificed. Knowing where you should be compromising when appointing the room will mean you will achieve what you really need to in the right areas and select furniture with the primary function in mind.

KEEP CLUTTER TO A MINIMUM

If practical, have a 'clear desk' policy. Work towards clearing all your work at the end of each day. This will stop the workspace from encroaching on the bedroom. Make this easier by using stylish, sizeable boxes to stow it all away. Versatile furniture helps; a bureau with a lift-up or roll-up door will hide the work paraphernalia. A desk concealed in a built-in cupboard works well also.

DIVIDING THE AREA

A psychological separation to divide the office and bedroom space is important. You want to be able to forget about your work once you've finished for the day, and softening the dominance of the desk within the room will help. Rather than a solid division like a screen, a subtle divide such a change in lighting can sometimes be enough. Using a table lamp in the desk area allows you to literally and metaphorically 'switch off' from work when you turn the light off. See pages 52–53 for ideas on how to screen off a desk area.

STYLE IT UP

If the desk area can't be hidden, ensure that everything that you do have on view is worthy of display. That means buying good-looking storage and keeping it uniform for a coherent look; a shelf of same-sized files, a row of identical boxes or a stack of prettily patterned boxes in co-ordinated shades looks so much better than a mishmash of shapes and dimensions. Then bring a bit of wit and character with carefully chosen accessories in a manner in keeping with the rest of the scheme of the room. Artworks, photos, pictures torn from magazines and your other treasures will all help create a personalised space that feels less like an office.

Working in bed

I sometimes like to work in bed. I might be reading, writing by hand, sketching or working on the laptop. In general it's a bad idea to keep work-related things by your bed as you simply won't be able to switch off, so I'm not going to suggest that you have a dedicated work table there, but rather that you allow yourself the flexibility to work in bed, if you're so inclined. A nest of tables is the perfect option. Use the top surface for your usual bedside stuff then, when you pull another table out, you've got the extra work surface space for piles of paperwork or books that would otherwise be on the floor. Another idea is to use a large tray to contain all your work - just as you would when having breakfast in bed. You can then simply carry it all back to the office when you've finished.

Why it works:
The bedroom/office

Not everyone has the space to dedicate to a fully-fledged home office. However, a comfortable workspace can be set up in most rooms of the house including a bedroom if necessary. This idea is successful when the two areas are clearly defined and one does not interfere with the other.

Hide it

Creating a division between the work and sleeping areas allows you to truly rest when you go to bed. A screen or 'mobile wall' is extremely useful in this situation. Alternatively use a piece of furniture to divide the zones. This could be a long low chest, a shelving unit or an open bookcase. Consider using two of the same bookcases positioned back to back – one side can be for clothes and the other for books and work-related paperwork. High open shelving is another option – as you don't have to fill every inch of it – so it will therefore retain some feeling of openness.

ZONING

A 'cocooning' headboard 'folds' round the bed, helping to define the bedroom space and acts as a mini screen, obscuring the view to the desk from the bed. The bedside cabinets add to this effect. When you're lying in bed, the room doesn't scream 'office'.

NON-OFFICEY

The key to making a bedroom-cum-office work isn't to whack in a great big office chair on wheels. The desk, chair and desk lamp link in with the feel of the other bedroom furniture. They have been chosen with a bedroom setting in mind first, office second. Nor is there anything too imposing on the desk; keeping everything low-level means you won't feel your work is towering over you at night. The wheels on the bedside cabinets mean they can easily move into the office area if needed.

GET THE FOCAL POINTS RIGHT

Create a focal point for your workstation – it's the view out of the window – facing away from the bed. That way you aren't sat staring at your bed all day. If you don't have a fabulous view, create a focal point using a painting or a moodboard, a cluster of your favourite treaures of the moment or a vase of flowers.

TEMPERATURE

For a decent night's sleep, the bedroom should be slightly cooler than the rest of the house at 18°C – whilst an office is more comfortable at 21°C. It's therefore important to be able to be able to vary the temperature of the room between night and day.

CLEAR DESK POLICY

For a sense of calm, stop the 'office' from intruding too much. This requires good storage. Choose non-officey files, folders and boxes to make the whole effect one of home rather than work.

Private passions

When you stop to think about it, maybe you don't need a home office. A laptop and a couple of files stowed away in a cupboard might be all the essentials required to keep the household running smoothly. Perhaps what's more important to you is that you have a place to sew or indulge a hobby? Allowing yourself space to indulge your passions is one of the nicest things you can do for yourself.

MAKING SPACE FOR YOUR CREATIVITY

✳ You don't have to dedicate a whole room or even corner of the room to accommodate your hobbies. I mentioned in Chapter One about 'lust-list must-lists' and how to make your dream a reality through comfortable compromise (see page 13). The same principle works here. Are you willing to scale back a little? Could you convert a piece of furniture to create a mini craft area as you would do for a desk area (see page 228)? Or turn a trunk or blanket box into your sewing hub using the kitchen table for the machine work?

✳ Think about a portable 'craft room'. I use a series of children's suitcases (see above) to store most of my craft kit, as I don't have space for a craft room just now. They're portable and it's really easy for me to grab one and take it to the sofa or kitchen table to work from whenever I want to.

✳ Take the stress out of wrapping, writing cards, thank you letters – these things quite rightly become a pleasure when you're set up to do them. Put together a box or a drawer of all the things you need including all the essentials.

✳ Having somewhere to curate your thoughts, passions and dreams is a joy. Harnessing and expressing them is step one of making them become real. The best way for you to do this depends on how you're hardwired, but I like to paste my ideas into sketchbooks and create 'dream boards' on the wall of my shed at the bottom of my garden (see opposite and left).

the BEDROOM

A bedroom is the most personal of retreats; a sanctuary and a haven. A very private space of comfort, restoration and healing. We spend an incredible portion of our lives in our bedrooms, (about a third if you're getting your full eight hours). Yet it is the part of the house that guests rarely see. In this sense, your bedroom provides you with the opportunity to create something truly for yourself. To get it right, you need to think about what it is you want from your bedroom. A good night's sleep, a morning in bed, a day in bed? Family lie ins and film nights, a love nest? All of the above? When do you spend time in there? Do you use the bedroom at other times during the day? Lie on your bed and let yourself consider and daydream, blending the reality of how you use the room with the fantasy of what you would like it to be.

Bedrooms can't operate on a totally ethereal level. As with any other room, there are technicalities that can be perfected to make it work well. It is no coincidence that we sleep well in wonderful hotels. Much time and consideration goes into the choices of mattress and lighting, and it is possible to take inspiration and ideas from this for a domestic setting.

Children's bedrooms are slightly different propositions. Buying for the long term is more difficult (but eminently possible) as their needs and tastes will change as they grow. They too need their personality reflected in their space, and the same sense of privacy and security that we expect ourselves.

For me, the bedroom is very much a night-time and first thing in the morning space, so I've put it together as the perfect place to induce sleep. In practice, that translates into a minimal and clutter-free room. My colour palette for my bedroom is very relaxing and calming; whites, greys, pales. It looks cosy at night with my heavy lined curtains and thick carpet, but it is light enough in the morning to make me want to get out of bed. Create what works best for you. Start with the basic and functional aspects and create your room around them.

Get a decent night's sleep

If you have ever had the good fortune to spend a night in a very smart hotel, you will be familiar with that very particular sort of magic that infuses the place, but most particularly, the bedrooms.

This memorable, restorative and fabulous experience is due to far more than a location, or the fact that you are removed from the everyday. The best hotel bedrooms are carefully and exactly crafted to deliver the upmost in sensuality and relaxation, and it's possible to replicate some of this in your home.

8 steps to a good night's sleep

In a top hotel, every element, from the size of the bed, the height of the bedside tables, the multi-layered window treatment, the exact positioning of the power sockets and the ease of reach of the controls for the bedside lights, has been thought about again and again until it's right. Unless you're starting your bedroom from scratch it's difficult to achieve this perfection, but there's still plenty you can do to create a restful, peaceful and soothing atmosphere and increase your chances of a decent night's sleep.

1 BUY THE BEST MATTRESS YOU CAN AFFORD
You really do get what you pay for. It's simple; a good mattress = a good night's sleep, which in turn means a happier you. See page 240 for tips on buying a bed and a mattress.

2 BLOCK OUT AS MUCH NOISE AND LIGHT AS YOU CAN
A quality pair of lined and interlined curtains will not only keep the sunlight from streaming into the room and waking you, but will help reduce noise pollution. And if your curtains have an extra layer of felt interlining, that will help even more. For more ideas on bedroom curtains, see pages 248–249. Soft surfaces in general tend to deaden noise levels – so layering a room with thick-pile carpet, upholstered chairs and headboad will all help to change the acoustic qualities in a room.

3 GET THE TEMPERATURE RIGHT
Not too hot, not too cold. How you like the temperature of your bedroom's a personal thing, but start at the average of 18°C and see how that feels. This is usually cooler than the other areas in your home, so you may need to turn down the radiators manually.

4 CHANGE THE BED REGULARLY
Ideally you should do this every ten days at a minimum. In our house it's become a Sunday ritual – the simple pleasure of getting into a bed with clean, ironed sheets after a hot bath seems an appropriate way to start a new week. For a linen water recipe to keep your linen smelling sweet, see page 47.

5 REMEMBER THE BEDROOM'S PRIMARY FUNCTION
A bedroom is a place for sleep and relaxation. Keep that in mind at every stage when putting your bedroom together. Choose colours to calm, furniture to comfort, textures to soothe. Consider your sensory response to everything you bring into you bedroom.

6 DECLUTTER
This is a point I often make and it needs to be said here again; declutter, declutter, declutter. The bedroom needs to be peaceful and to me that means a room that's clear of bits and bobs, piles of clothes and so forth. To achieve that decluttered effect, you'll need to provide enough storage.

7 KEEP THINGS SMELLING SWEET
Once you've blocked out noise and light, turn your attention to your sense of smell. Keep your bedroom door closed if you're cooking a meal with strong odours as the scent can linger and disturb your sleep. Calming fragrances such as lavender, neroli and camomile will all aid relaxation. A little drop on a cotton wool ball popped into your pillowcase is all you need. See pages 134–139 for more ideas on scent.

8 FEEL SAFE AND SOUND
Think about where you position your bed and which side of the bed you prefer to sleep. Both of these influence your sense of security in bed and this, in turn, will affect the quality of your sleep. You should also instill a family culture of the 'sanctuary' of the bedroom and that means always knocking and waiting before entering.

Piecing together the bedroom

Pick a bed for the love of it: choose for real comfort to suit your body and choose for the sort of looks that make you happy as your bed will both dominate and define the style of your bedroom.

THE BED

✳ Size is all important. Buy the biggest bed you can fit into the room with enough space around to be practical for bedside tables and for changing the bedlinen. This should be about 60cm to 90cm on three of the four sides.

✳ Your bed should suit your signature style. There are five generic styles (see right). Don't feel limited by the volume of your room – a four-poster can work well in a relatively small space as its scale and height can make the room feel more roomy.

✳ While size matters, the mattress matters more. You really do get what you pay for with a mattress, so buy the most luxurious and well made one you can afford.

✳ It is an absolute must to go and lie down on several types of mattress and stores are well used to this ritual. If you are a couple, go shopping together as you need to lie down together for several minutes (however embarrassing). Make sure you lie in a few different ways, particularly in your preferred sleep position to get a proper idea of how the mattress really feels.

✳ A headboard will finish off a divan bed and make it more of a focal point, lending it the importance and impact it deserves within the space. Not least, a headboard adds comfort. There are masses of ready-made headboards on the market, so you should have no problem finding one that you like.

Choosing a mattress

✳ Among the many types, there are box spring mattresses, memory foam mattresses, feather mattresses and cashmere and silk-padded mattresses. Generally, the more comfortable and certainly more expensive mattresses have thicker padding, higher coil counts and a cushion sewn into the mattress.

✳ Know what the bed base is before you purchase the mattress. A mattress on a sprung divan base can be more firm than a mattress that is going to be partnered with a bed that has pine slats for a base.

✳ Look for deeper mattresses (22–30cm inbetween the seams) as sagging in a mattress is generally caused by insufficient padding, not defective or weak wire coils.

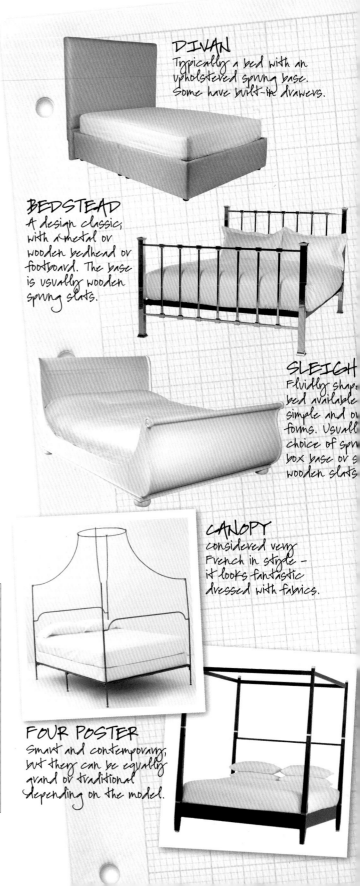

DIVAN Typically a bed with an upholstered spring base. Some have built-in drawers.

BEDSTEAD A design classic, with a metal or wooden bedhead or footboard. The base is usually wooden sprung slats.

SLEIGH Fluidly shaped bed available in simple and ornate forms. Usually a choice of sprung box base or wooden slats.

CANOPY considered very French in style – it looks fantastic dressed with fabrics.

FOUR POSTER Smart and contemporary, but they can be equally grand or traditional depending on the model.

Dressing up the bed

✳ This is where your signature style can come into play and you can experiment with colours, a mix of patterns and use of texture.

✳ Pay attention to the bedspread as this is the simplest way to make the bed look neat when you are not sleeping in it. Either spread it out completely to cover the entire bed – or fold in half to cover just the bottom section of the bed. Alternatively, fold it to form a runner to place across the middle of the bed.

✳ Avoid having too many dress cushions as they inevitably end up on the floor or taking up too much space on the bed, meaning you get less space for a comfortable night's sleep. Also, boys dislike them as they get in their way.

BEDSIDE TABLES

Bedside tables need not be 'bedside tables' – an upright dining chair or stool, a trunk or nest of tables plus many other items can all be used. Generally, for ease of use, you want a bedside to be the same height as your mattress, but it's very personal (I like mine a little taller). Don't worry about things being too matchy-matchy. It's okay to have two different bedside tables, and the lamps don't have to match either.

To avoid the clutter that can accumulate it's useful to place a pretty box or lidded container on the bedside table to stow away the pills, cuticle cream and other bits and bobs.

If space is limited a shallow shelf will give you enough room for the basics such a glass of water, a book and a radio. Then use a floor lamp or a wall light instead of a table lamp.

DRESSING TABLES

A dressing table is a luxury, but they are very much back in vogue not only because they are practical places to sit and finish dressing (hair, make-up, accessories and jewellery), but they provide additional display and storage for your personal things. If there is very little space in your bedroom, a slim, floating shelf can work as an option for holding a vanity mirror, hairdryer and brush, perfume, jewellery and other nick-nacks.

DAY BEDS, CHAISES, ARMCHAIRS AND BENCHES

A day bed, chaise, chair or bench at the end of the bed is the perfect place to perch for taking off your shoes, painting your toenails and so forth. If you think you'll be sitting on it with no clothes on, make sure it's a warm, cushioned surface rather than metal or wood.

MIRRORS

A large floor-to-ceiling mirror can turn the area around your wardrobe into a 'dressing area'. It will also reflect light into the room and help to give the illusion of more space – and obviously, big mirrors look great too.

Alternative bedside tables

✳ A tower of books brings an element of fun.

✳ A chair with a few hardback books to level the surface is a practical option.

Alternative headboards

← Hang a mirror. Go for one the same width as the bed.

A decorative textile such as an embroidered blanket or a patchwork quilt will warm and soften the bedroom as well as provide a focal point.

Hang patterned wallpaper or a graphic square or rectangle.

Clothes storage

Most of us are guilty of hoarding far too many clothes. If they are stuffed in drawers or not hung or organised properly, they invariably get forgotten about. Make your clothes work for you by utilising effective, stylish storage.

✳ Start by doing an inventory of everything you need to store in the bedroom. It makes sense to declutter now at this point.
✳ Then look at the best ways to store these items. How much hanging and folded storage do your clothes require? How often will you need to access them?
✳ Prioritise your storage according to how easy it is to access it – then organise your clothes accordingly. Prime space; a rail within arm's reach in the wardrobe or the top drawer in a chest of drawers should be given over to items you need to get to everyday.
✳ Being able to see your clothes properly will make mornings run more smoothly – so don't ram clothes too tightly into a wardrobe.
✳ It's important for storage to support the flow of activity of dressing. This is especially important if there are two of you trying to make it out of the house at the same time.
✳ Get into the habit of seasonal rotation to free up prime drawer and hanging space.

*Hooks positioned on the inside of wardrobe and cupboard doors (see above) make use of otherwise lost space. It's the perfect place for ties, scarves or belts.

*Bespoke fitted storage (see below left) maximises space and provides the correct ratios of storage types you specifically need. Glass-fronted storage (see right) requires discipline or it can easily become messy. Storage can be dual-function. A chest of drawers (see below) doubles as a bedside table.

3 ways to keep the moths at bay

1 The key to keeping moths at bay is to launder all out-of-season items before putting them away into storage. It's also important to spring clean all your drawers and cupboards to get rid of dust.
2 Store your valuable clothes in sealable garment bags within a trunk or a chest so that moths won't be able to get to them, but take the clothes out every few months to air.
3 Place a cotton wool ball with a few drops of clove, lavender or cedar essential oil in with the clothes to help repel moths.

Girlie treasures

You don't have to keep all your hats, scarves, jewellery etc., hidden behind closed doors. Let them earn their keep by displaying them on view and incorporating them into part of your décor. It's the equivalent of having your pretty dinner service on display in the dining room. Look to high-end clothes shops and boutiques for inspiration – many of their merchandising tricks can be translated into your bedroom.

CLOTHES

✳ Fix door knobs, hooks and other interesting 'hangers' to the wall to give yourself more opportunity to display your things (as shown below).

✳ Go for the unexpected. Hats stacked one on top of the other on a bust or miniature statue is very amusing because it is so tongue in cheek. It's always good to have a surprise like that in your personal space as it will away make you smile.

✳ Take things up a notch by using decorative hangers; padded fabric covered, embellished with beads, antique wood or wire ones fashioned into wonderful shapes.

✳ Think of clothes as art and as an installation on the wall – one amazing kimono or sparkly dress or even a humble linen dress is going to look wonderful hanging from a hook.

Jewellery display

✳ Take the opportunity to go through your jewellery box and pull out things you want to see all the time – even if you don't want to wear them.

✳ Small trays are a great way to contain and tidy all the little pieces. Use small boxes, teacups or jars to organise everything.

✳ Small evening bags look great when hung like a series of pictures on the wall – and that way they are always easy to grab when you need them.

✳ One of the nicest ways to display jewellery is to cover it with a bell jar or cloche – it keeps the dust off, but also raises the perceived value as it's behind glass as if it were in a museum. Always remember displays can constantly be changed.

*Be controlled when you are styling; remember you are creating a display not confusional mess.

*Think laterally; one of your grandmother's teacups (or one you picked up in a junk shop) is the perfect holder for jewellery (see right).

*A pair of antlers (see left) is an unexpected way to display pretty dresses.

*It's delightful to hang necklaces you long to see, but rarely wear onto an equally ornate chandelier (see left)

*A cluster of brooches (see opposite, top) pinned to a cushion will give it a new lease of life.

Light in the bedroom

Study the natural light in your room so you can work out how to dress the windows to suit you. At the same time, make sure you have good bedside lights for reading that can be angled or dimmed when you want more gentle light levels.

Daylight

Make the most of it as there is nothing more uplifting than filtered sunlight filling your bedroom during the day. However, for some, there is nothing more annoying than being woken up by streaming sunshine at dawn.

NATURAL WINDOW TREATMENTS

✳ Design to suit you. Think in terms of flexible window treatments especially if you want to both let in and block out natural light, particularly on very sunny days. This flexibility will work whether you want to snooze in the afternoon, allow the light to stream through in the morning or sleep in a completely darkened room.

✳ Semi-sheer blinds, venetian blinds or shutters will all give you privacy while allowing some light into the room; equally, semi-sheer fabric curtains in voile, cotton or linen will all filter daylight to create a dreamy quality of light in the space. They also give you some privacy during the day.

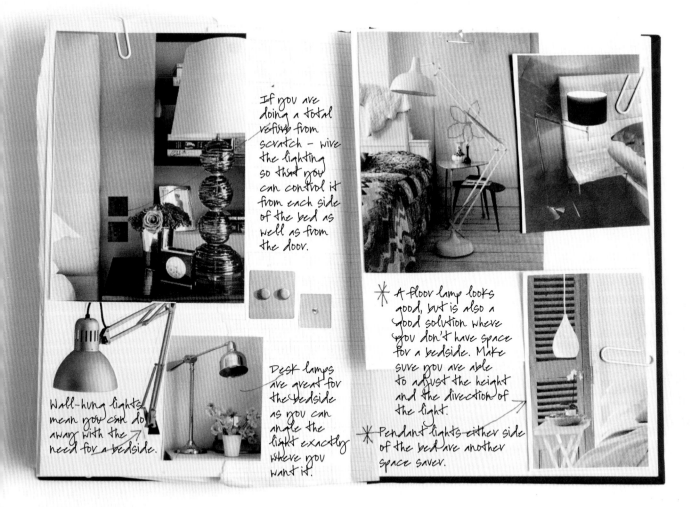

If you are doing a total refurb from scratch – wire the lighting so that you can control it from each side of the bed as well as from the door.

* A floor lamp looks good, but is also a good solution where you don't have space for a bedside. Make sure you are able to adjust the height and the direction of the light.

* Pendant lights either side of the bed are another space saver.

Wall-hung lights mean you can do away with the need for a bedside.

Desk lamps are great for the bedside as you can angle the light exactly where you want it.

* A well made pair of lined and interlined curtains will not only keep out natural daylight, but will also help reduce noise at night when they are closed and make the room feel very cozy. Lined curtains are two layer curtains of fabric and lining. Interlined curtains have three layers – fabric, interlining and lining. Blackout curtains can be three layers of fabric, blackout interlining and lining, or even four layers of fabric, interlining, blackout lining and lining.

* Curtains should be measured very accurately in terms of length (so they just kiss the ground and do not look ill-fitting or cheap) and width (so there is enough fullness of fabric plus sufficient overhang on either sides and the middle to avoid any annoying 'cracks' of light blazing through in the mornings).

Artificial light

In an ideal world, lights in the bedroom would be controlled from both sides of the bed and from the doorway, but to achieve this means a total re-wire. Here's how to light your bedroom without the hassle.

WAYS TO LIGHT THE BEDROOM

* You need to be able to reach out as you drift off to sleep and switch off your bedside light with ease. A good choice is a light with an inline on–off switch or a touch-sensitive light that switches on and off when you touch the lampshade.

* Avoid glare from the bulb when you're reading in bed; choose the right height lamp for your table and for the height of your bed. The idea is that you can't see a bare bulb from the bed.

* Don't worry about matching the light fittings either side. I have an adjustable metal desk lamp on one side and a classic Empire-style black glass lamp base with a black silk shade at the other.

* If you are a bit short of space on your bedside table, don't go for a table lamp at all. Instead install a pendant lamp (allowing 30cm between the bottom of the shade and the table), a wall-hung fitting or an adjustable floor lamp that allows you to direct the light where you need it.

* The dressing table is the place where your lighting can be decorative as well as functional. Choose a light that appeals to you. As long as it gives enough light for applying make-up (assuming that's where you do it) anything goes.

* We all know the beauty that candles can bring to a room, but never ever use them when there's the slightest chance you may fall asleep and leave them burning – it's just not worth the risk.

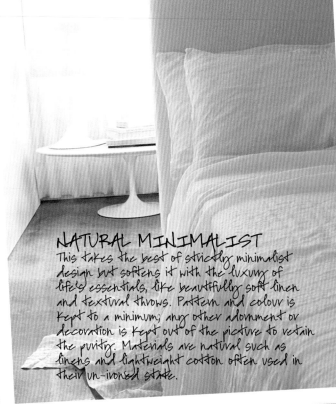

NATURAL MINIMALIST

This takes the best of strictly minimalist design but softens it with the luxury of life's essentials, like beautifully soft linen and textural throws. Pattern and colour is kept to a minimum; any other adornment or decoration is kept out of the picture to retain the purity. Materials are natural such as linens and lightweight cotton often used in their un-ironed state.

BOHEMIAN

This is a typically free mix where almost anything goes as long as you personally love it. The characteristics of a bohemian look is that it's totally liberated from most design rules. Mix it up – bohemian can mean global, chintzy, modern and graphic, girlie or retro.

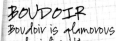

BOUDOIR

Boudoir is glamorous and girlie. It's a seductive space that's intimate and slightly risqué. Luxury textures like silks and satins are vital components.

HOTEL SHARP

This is the slickest most streamlined of bedroom looks that has a masculine feeling. Starched cotton sheets are the base on which the colour is added and this style really allows you to use large blocks of strong colour.

Choosing your bedlinen

The choice is huge. As well as practicality, consider the overall feel and look that you are trying to achieve. Do you love crisp white hotel-style sheets (high thread count white cotton) or are you after something that says a little more about your signature style (layers of pattern)? Don't think that your choice of bedding stops at the 'linen'. There are throws, blankets and cushions to consider too.

When choosing bedlinen, apply the same rules as when you are finding your signature style. Think about the 'feel' each piece conjures up. Your bedroom is a very special place and the bed is its key feature. It will pay you to get it right (see left).

The sheets, pillows and duvet covers
COTTON
* In my view nothing comes close to crisp white sheets, but there's more to choose from than just plain white; there are subtle patterns too, like a self-stripe, a jacquard and a checked weave (see page 94).
* To look its best pure cotton will need to be ironed, but you can buy polycotton which can be shaken out (avoiding all the ironing).
* It is easy to bring in some colour or additional colour with bordered or piped pillowcases or pillows in solid colours that go in the mix with your otherwise plain white bedlinen. This will break up the all-white scheme without affecting its purity.

Hospital corners? Why bother?
Because it means you don't need to iron the bottom sheet – a trick an interior designer friend taught me. Pulling the sheet tight flattens out all the creases. While this lets you off the ironing-the-bottom-sheet hook, it is absolutely, totally and utterly worth the effort to iron everything else – top sheet, duvet cover and pillowcases. Those perfectly ironed crisp sheets are another reason hotel rooms are so delicious.

LINEN
* Pure linen is a dream to sleep on, but for many of us the work involved is too great. There are, though, excellent washed or 'softened' linens that look good in their slightly rumpled state. They are particularly suitable in a relaxed (or rustic) environment (see opposite).
* If you have a crisp throw at the end of a bed and use a couple of scatter cushions it will still look neat.
* When you wash this softened linen, pull it tight and fold it dry to take as much of the work out of changing the bed as possible.
SILK
* Glamorous and girlie, but choose the colour carefully, opt for muted tones as they look classier. Wash, wash and wash again before you sleep on silk sheets for the first time as this process takes away the 'slip'.
* To some it is no myth that sleeping on silk pillowcases helps keep wrinkles at bay and improves the sheen of your hair.
PATTERN
* Pattern can be country, art deco, bohemian, modernist, classic, hippy – choose it to suit your eye.
* When you mix pattern on your bed, stick to a colour palette and mix the pattern up a bit so it doesn't look like a matching set. There's always room for some plain in the mix.

The accessories
* Don't overdo the decorative pillows. Never have more than three.
* Blankets are your best friends in terms of colour – you can never have enough of them to take you through the seasons. A throw at the bottom of the bed is an ideal finishing touch and is very practical and useful. See page 241 for more ideas on dressing the bed.

*If you are fitting a valance, make sure it just kisses the ground (see far left) so it does not look cheap or ill-fitting. Search online for companies who make to order so that you can get the size just right. Kick pleats at the corners are smart and modern and not at all old fashioned.

Why it works: A calm yet colourful bedroom

Colour and pattern, whether bold or quiet, brings life to a scheme; but in the bedroom it's important to remember the primary function is relaxation, but that doesn't have to mean boring and drab – balance function and style.

LIGHTS

A pair of swivel-arm wall lights may be an unusual choice for a bedroom but they are immensely practical – giving off enough light to read by without any glare from a naked bulb.

WINDOW

A double-layered window treatment of curtains plus a sheer panel next to the window gives the best of both worlds – privacy as well as light. The yellow dip-dye at the bottom of the curtains picks out the accent colour of yellow in the wallpaper, as does the seat cushion on the chair.

STORAGE

A niche built into the wall provides bedside storage without a bedside table. It also makes the walk-in wardrobe layout possible – a bedside would restrict access to this.

CHAIR

The dark colour of this chair blends with the flooring so that it doesn't overpower the room when viewed from the bed. The curved shape takes up less space than a blocky chair and is much easier to pass with its rounded edges.

FLOATING WALL

A floating wall built 90cm from the existing wall hides a walk-in wardrobe behind the bed. All storage and associated clutter are hidden well out of sight. The patterned wallpaper acts as an alternative to a headboard and creates the focal point in the room. The skirting board fitted to the bottom of the floating wall helps turn it into an architectural feature.

DRESSING THE BED

Large square pillows easily provide enough comfort for sitting up in bed reading, despite there not being a headboard. An all white bed is a clean crisp contrast to the dark carpet and makes the 'retro' wallpaper feel modern rather than traditional.

USING COLOUR IN THE BEDROOM

Colour and pattern is totally subjective – it all comes down to personal taste and preference. One person's décor of patterned walls and deep coloured carpet (their warm and inviting) might be enough to bring out a headache and insomnia in another. The most important rule to follow when choosing colour and pattern for your bedroom is to remember the primary function is to sleep...keep things to your version of the perfect sleep-inducing bedroom.

The guest room

A guest room is a unique opportunity; a chance to shape and create a beautiful space for your visitors, unencumbered by your own needs or possessions. You can indulge yourself and your guests with your own interpretation of a haven and a retreat. Dress this room with notions of comfort, hospitality and privacy.

ENSURING A GOOD NIGHT'S SLEEP FOR YOUR GUESTS

Aspire to offering your guests the same standard as you enjoy in your own bedroom. If you can, make the guest room (if it's a dedicated space) even more clutter-free than your room. Think of the best hotel room you've ever stayed in. Test your guest room out at least once so you know what your friends and family will experience. A trial run or two gives you an opportunity to iron out any problems.

TOWELS AND BEDLINEN

The non-negotiables are fresh towels and fresh linen. If you want to save a little of the hassle, there's nothing wrong with making the bed

with a top sheet under the duvet; that way you can just change the sheets and pillowcases and not have to change the duvet cover every time.

WARM IT UP

Have extra blankets or throws available and on show – one person's cool and unstuffy means an arctic chill for another. I sometimes slip a hot water bottle into the bottom of the bed in winter as a nice surprise.

BOIL IT UP

I don't bother putting a kettle in the room unless my guests are bringing a bottle-fed baby; being able to warm up a bottle with ease in the middle of the night is of benefit to everyone in the house.

TV OR NOT TV?

I'm not big on TVs in bedrooms and I certainly don't put them in guest rooms. Why are they in their room watching TV when they've come to spend quality time with you? Retreating to the bedroom for a moment's quiet before dinner, fine. Staying there catching up on the latest HBO series, not so fine.

KIDS' NIGHTS OUT

If you've got lots of children coming, encourage them to bring sleeping bags and a roll mat. They'll see it as fun and it will save you a lot of trouble.

Children's bedrooms: Nursery

A nursery is a very special room, especially so if it is for a very first baby. It is a truly curious and enchanting experience to decorate and beautify a space for a soon-to-arrive baby. A project to be savoured and enjoyed, it is a wonderfully personal and uplifting aspect of the many preparations that take place before welcoming your child into the world.

THINK OF MUM
The design of the nursery has to be just as much for the mother as the baby. Getting the nursery room ready is very much a part of the psychological preparation for your first child. I would suggest that where space permits that you do always have a bed in the nursery as you do not know how the first months will go, but you can be sure that there will be many interrupted nights and all mothers need some kind of place to lie or sit quietly when this happens. You might choose to have a sofa or a comfortable feeding chair in place of a bed.

FUTURE PROOFING
It is a given that you must design any children's space so that it can evolve – children grow up very quickly. It is therefore sensible to invest in classics that will last through the first ten years or so. A single cot bed (with removable sides) will take most children through to the age of eight or so. You do not need to invest in a specially designed changing table when you can use a chest of drawers just as easily (changing does not have to be done in the baby's room when you can just as easily do this in the bathroom).

STORAGE
During the early years, most baby and child clothing is easier to fold away into drawers than to hang, so make sure you have plenty of drawer space. Hang really special outfits (always presents from doting friends) that are too cute to put away on miniature hangers and hooks so they are very much on show.

DÉCOR
Calming and harmonious colours always work well in a nursery – pastel tones that are almost white like soft pink, watery blue and muted green. But in larger, predominantly white rooms, blocks of colour can work (see right). Fitting a dimmer switch is essential, so you can control light levels and see your baby without waking them, as are blackout roller blinds behind the curtains, or blackout-lined curtains so that the baby can sleep in absolute darkness.

*A changing station can come in handy, but if there's space in the bathroom – locate it there instead of the bedroom. A strip of colour painted on the wall of the room in an otherwise minimalist space (see above) creates a 'headboard' feel for each of the cots.

Children's bedrooms: Toddler/school

COMING TO TERMS WITH THEIR 'TASTE'

Kids seem to love the bright and the gaudy, but it is a stage that only really lasts for a few years. If you give your young children the chance to be involved in the 'making home' process, they will generally respond with enormous enthusiasm and devise wonderful ideas (however utterly impractical).

STYLING

Of course you must let your children arrange their special and favourite things in their rooms – there will be the soft toys, squidgy-faced animals and a whole host of soldiers, fairies and other 'essentials' but the point is to give children the time and opportunity to be involved, so they feel as though they have been part of making the space special to them. That way you are, almost by default, teaching them how to look after and love their rooms, which in itself is a marvellous skill to have.

DÉCOR

Each and every item in a child's bedroom will be perceived as being a toy of some sort. The sidewinder on the blind (fantastic grinding noise), the curtains (swing city) and the chest of drawers (hide and seek; pull out beds for the dolls and battlefields for the toys). Therefore always purchase with robustness in mind and design window treatments with care. In terms of layout, my advice would be to choose one wall that can take a number of shelves or alcove storage and paint this in a single bright blue, pink, purple or green (to suit your child's eye for colour) and make this their display/storage area. You will be surprised by how you can make almost anything look good when all the various items are grouped together in this way

STORAGE

Drawer space for clothes is still the most pratical clothes storage, so there's no need for a wardrobe yet. One of the best ways to store soft toys is to give them their own hammock that is wall-mounted. It is very practical, and the hammock becomes yet another toy in the space.

*Children under the age of seven do not need much hanging space – drawer space is still more practical and a row of hooks on the wall is sufficient for the school uniform during the week and for girls, prettier kit at the weekends.

Children's bedrooms:
The teen years

A teenager's room needs to evolve as he or she grows. It is very important to let them have the lead in how their room will look as it is their room and you want them to take responsibility for it. While you will be providing the basics of bed, wardrobe, chest, a desk and chair and probably some shelving, the way the space is appointed should be decided by the person sleeping and living in it.

PRIVACY

From about the age of 11 to 12 years old, most children will want everyone to knock on their bedroom door before entering (if they allow entrance at all). Privacy is a basic right and should be respected. This is nothing to worry about as it is just a bid for independence to keep siblings out and is probably not directed at you as the parent. Respect their desire for privacy, but make some clear rules about who is keeping the room clean and make it clear that the cleaner is going to be admitted.

DÉCOR

As a parent, you will already have provided the basics in terms of furniture, but the actual design look of the room should be largely decided by your young adult offspring. It is a wise decision to let them choose from existing furniture or, if you are buying new, involve them in the choices (it makes them feel as though they have some control). Once you have found some common ground it is relatively easy to put together a look, just as you would in any other room in the house. It is always a good idea to buy a huge and/or colourful spread for the bed for both boys or girls. The bed is the centre of a teenage room – at times a beauty salon, play station, study area and chill space. The bedspread will protect against inevitable ink stains, nail polish, tea and coffee and undoubtedly more...

FURNITURE

You can really help your child by making sure that the room is restful for sleep and comfortable for homework. Space permitting, I would suggest that you give them a double bed. This is the time to buy a decent bed, because up until the 'double digit' years you can always get away with improving single beds with mattress toppers. On principle, install a desk with a good lamp and comfortable chair because teenage years are as much about study as anything else (despite what they say). I would avoid allowing a television in a teen room as this, like laptops and phones, eats into sleeping time.

*Completely accept that teenagers love to stick posters, pictures and other mementos onto their walls with whatever is to hand – it's part of their self-expression and it is as important for them as teens to be able to do this, as it is for a five year old child to let their imagination take them off into their own worlds.

the BATHROOM

What do you need your bathroom to do for you? Do you love a long bedtime soak or is it used for rushed morning showers? Does it have to be multi-functional; is it a place for getting clean as well as a playroom for the kids, a home spa and a haven for the adults of the household too?

There are ways to improve on what you have without taking drastic action and ripping out the whole space. Whether you are simply sprucing up the bathroom you have, or working towards a complete overhaul, begin by removing the clutter and doing a deep clean. Even a basic standard bathroom looks inviting when it's clean and sparkly, and it may even delay the need for a full rework. Bathrooms are unfairly perceived as clinical, sterile, functional spaces. Bring artworks in, furniture that you don't think of as conventionally 'bathroomy'. Treat it as you would any other room and give it the same consideration and flair. Lighting is important; you need the flexibility to be able to dim, relax and switch off from the harsh glare of bright bulbs; this is key to creating that spa feel at home. Indulge in some luxury bathing basics; a pile of towels, generous amounts of soaps, new flannels. As with any other room, curtains, a gorgeous colour on the walls, pattern and ornate light fittings can all be brought into the bathroom. The downstairs lavatory is a public space which most visitors will see. It's also the room that doesn't need to be seriously or traditionally decorated. Feel at liberty to reveal a flash of eccentricity here – it's just a way of showing a little bit of you.

7 tips for a bathroom overhaul

Even a plain basic white bathroom can be made into something pretty special with very little expense or hassle. Here's how...

1 Remove and clean away all your products and accessories – everything. Put them in a big cardboard box (you'll sort through that later) and give the room a really good clean from top to bottom.

2 Paint, scrub and renew. If painted walls and woodwork are looking grubby, it's time for another coat of paint (in a new colour perhaps?). Scrub any grouting that's looking grim – there are specialist grout cleaning products on the market if you need them. If cleaning fails, re-grout. The silicone seals between the bath or shower and the tiling are another problem area. Renew any that are looking past their best.

3 Edit. Then, it's about bringing back an edited version of what you had before, adding in a few new accessories and styling it up. Sort through your boxes of products and get rid of anything that you haven't used in a long time or that's past its best (once open, beauty products have a shelf life, after which their active ingredients lose their potency).

4 Store. This is key to avoiding a mishmash of bottles. Keep the good-looking things (the glamorous Christmas and birthday presents of bath oils, scrubs, creams and bath salts) out on display and provide plenty of space to stow the rest away. Hooks, rails, rods and racks all make great storage devices and help make use of the back of the door and wall space. Think, too, about accessibility; you'll need a hook for a towel that's within arm's reach of the shower and maybe a tray of lotions near the bath.

5 Upgrade your basics. Buy a pile of new towels and two new bath mats (one on the floor and one in the wash), and relegate any worn or grey ones to the cupboard under the sink/the garage for drying the dog/cleaning engine oil off your hands/mopping kitchen floor spills. (For tips on buying towels and looking after them, see pages 96–97). I prefer white towels, but it's useful to have a couple of large dark ones (for hair dying or a fake tan applying night). It's also a good idea to have a dark coloured face towel or flannel for make-up removal so that pure white ones don't get ruined.

6 Improve the lighting by fitting a dimmer. Low-level ambient lighting will hide a multitude of sins (see page 270 for lighting ideas) and is the only way that you'll get a home spa feel. There are even dimmers available that can be fitted to a pull cord within the bathroom. Light candles at night, too.

7 Add the finishing touches. Pot up a plant or bring in a small vase of flowers. If you're short of space, keep the flower stems short and the vase squat so you don't risk knocking it all over. (See page 266 for more bathroom styling ideas).

Flash the cash

If your bathroom is a complete disaster zone (avocado suite, poor plumbing, 1970s patterned tiles, to name just a few of the horrors I inherited in my bathroom) save up your money, rip the whole lot out and start again from scratch. No amount of styling genius is going to make up for problems like these. This is one room in the house where it really pays to buy yourself out of a problem.

Treat it like any other room

Bathrooms needn't be at all clinical. Employ the same creativity as you would elsewhere to make the most of your bathing space.

MIX THINGS UP

Don't feel you have to buy everything from the place where you buy the bathroom suite. Instead, think like a hunter-gatherer. Use accessories like the loo roll holder, towel rails, hooks and mirror as a chance to add your personal style.

BRING IN UNCONVENTIONAL FURNITURE

It's pure luxury to have a comfortable chair for someone to sit in and chat to you while you soak or for you to lounge in after a bath. Some pieces can be extremely practical as well as looking the part. A chest of drawers provides great storage for towels, spare boxes of tissues and those creams in less than glamorous packaging, but also doubles as a dressing table and a perch for all your pretty potions and lotions.

STYLE IT UP

Decorative accessories like art, ornate mirrors and pretty storage all have a place in the bathroom because, in effect, they are the final layer of colour in conjunction with your (possibly considerable) bathing and beauty products. The absolute final layer of colour, of course, comes in the form of flowers...

*Orchids are the perfect plant for a bathroom as they enjoy taking their moisture from the air and flower for a considerable number of weeks.

Mirror, mirror

Bathroom mirrors don't just have to be practical – for shaving, tweezing eyebrows or applying make-up. They can also be used to increase light levels, help make the bathroom appear bigger than it really is (the bigger the mirror, the better) and can be used to bring a decorative element to the room. In fact, mirrors are a cheap way to up the ante in an otherwise plain scheme and you can take them with you if you move.

Make your own sink console

Firstly, you must have the help of a carpenter/plumber to make this idea work as well as it should. When you are buying the sink and taps, make sure there is sufficient length on the taps to reach over the height of the sink. You will need to drill two holes in the top of the table – one for the sink waste and the other for the taps. Choose a metal bottle trap as this will be seen from most angles and a white plastic one will cheapen the whole effect.

Bathroom colours and soft furnishings

In any other room, you would consider the colours and soft furnishings vital components of your décor. When designing a bathroom, we tend to get hung up on the practicalities, so these aren't the first things that spring to mind. But layering pattern, colour and texture will personalise the space, and turn it into a room you'll truly enjoy.

THE COLOUR PALETTE

Bathrooms don't have to be restricted to off-whites and other neutral tones, in fact the bathroom is an excellent place to bring in real colour – it's a self-contained space so needn't be part of the colour scheme of the rest of your home. Dark, moody colours work just as well as the more obvious watery blue palette, providing the bathroom's well lit. For instance, midnight blue, teal and dark grey add depth and atmosphere to a bathroom that's well endowed with natural and artificial light and that has plenty of mirrors. The water in the bath only adds to the effect.

USING WALLPAPER

Wallpaper and moisture are never going to be best friends, but it is possible to use wallpaper in WCs and large bathrooms if there's good ventilation. Avoid it though, in small bathrooms with power showers. It's always advisable to seal the wallpaper with two coats of matt acrylic varnish. You will also need to protect vulnerable areas of wallpaper adjacent to the sink or bath. It's your choice to use a few rows of tiles as a splashback or you could use clear acrylic sheeting cut to size and screwed to the wall. Seal the edges of the acrylic discreetly with silicone to make it watertight.

CURTAINS AND BLINDS
There's no reason why you can't bring fabrics into a bathroom with good ventilation – just as you would anywhere else.

SOMETHING UNEXPECTED
A decorative solid screen is a great alternative window treatment. It brings warmth and substance to a bathroom.

SHUTTERS – louvred shutters make it easy to control light levels so you can get that spa-like ambience during the day. They also offer total privacy.

FROSTED GLASS AND FILM
Switching over your old-fashioned textured glass to plain frosted glass transforms a window. Frosted film is the closest you'll get – and it's easy to apply.

Secret Shell. 2.

Fabrics in the bathroom

You don't have to be restricted to what you'd normally think of as 'bathroom-safe' furnishings. Most fabrics will survive in a bathroom with good ventilation and/or windows that open. See it as an opportunity to add a bit of decoration or an element of luxe.

* Avoid silk and velvet and stick to tough natural fabrics such as cotton and linen. Linen is super-tough. In fact, it's stronger wet than dry so will last a lot longer than other natural fabrics.

* Rather than making interlined curtains, keep things simple so that you can wash them easily. A double layer of fabric (pre-washed so it doesn't shrink on the first wash) will give enough bulk and privacy. Choose simple fixings to attach the curtain to a pole; ties, clips or eyelets are all washing machine friendly.

* If privacy isn't an issue – a sheer linen voile blind may be an option – they filter the light beautifully.

* If you like a spa-like ambience in your bathroom, being able to control the amount of light that comes in is key. You could add a layer of blackout lining to a blind or curtain to allow you to create a night-time experience at any time of day.

* If you have space to bring in a comfortable chair it's more practical to choose one with loose covers that can be removed and washed. You could always make your own loose cover from towelling fabric or by stitching a patchwork of patterned towels together.

ON THE FLOOR

Rugs and runners make good alternatives to traditional bathmats and are an easy way to add colour to an all-white bathroom. Flat weave cotton designs are the most practical as they dry out quickly after use. Choose ones that are small enough to fit in the washing machine, but large enough to soak up any splashes from a shower.

THE SHOWER CURTAIN

One of the nicest ways to make an ordinary plastic shower curtain into something special is to back it with a fabric that you love. My choice would be antique French linen, but stripes or flashy florals would also look delightful. Either use a ready-made fabric curtain or make your own panel and hang it from the same shower rail with rings, ties or clips.

You don't have to use a standard plastic shower rail either. Instead, consider the same options that are open to you in the lounge or the bedroom; thick chunky wooden curtain rails or sleek minimalist metal poles will all work – many of these are available with both wall and ceiling fittings.

Lighting your bathroom

Balance and control is key to lighting the bathroom, but try not to be seduced by state of the art costly systems, as there are ways of working with an existing lighting circuit to good effect.

TASK LIGHTING

It really matters that you can see yourself properly when you need too, which is why you need some form of task light directed to the bathroom mirror. If your current lighting is not sufficient for shaving or applying make-up, then you should consider employing an electrician to fit additional lights, to the existing circuit, some of which should be directional, and all controlled with a dimmer switch. If this is not an option because your bathroom has a single central light electrical feed, then you can fit a surface-mounted bathroom light that has three or four directional spotlights which can also be controlled by a dimmer switch. This means you can direct two or even three of the spots to the mirror, while the other can be pointed in a different direction.

ADDING GLAMOUR

Other stylish lighting, such as a light on a side table (as long as it is well away from the bath; check current regulations with your electrician) or a graceful chandelier will make your bathroom feel much more special and liveable. Remember to think big as large scale pieces will work wonders even in smaller spaces.

DIMMING THE LIGHTS

It is usually possible to fit a dimmer for a bathroom, especially when the switch is outside the room (the usual position these days). Where you have a pull cord fitting within the bathroom, ask your electrician if he can chase the wire through from the bathroom to the outside wall as in many instances this is easily possible with minimal expense and mess (though there is always redecoration to be done).

CANDLES

Candle light is wonderfully flattering and casts a great mood on both the room and you. Several candles will give you enough light by which to bathe, but they give you more than that if they are lightly scented with natural oils like jasmine, rose and lavender. Choose relaxing scents that you particularly love and, where possible, buy candles that are scented with essential oils as they are more gentle on the senses and imbue well-being and calm.

Upping the ante in the bathroom

Whether it's a little DIY pampering that you're in need of or you've got guests coming to stay for the weekend, here's how to make your bathroom feel a little special.

TURNING IT INTO A SPA

✳ It actually takes very little. The biggest hurdle is to commit to taking time out to pamper yourself in the first place.

✳ Start with a pile of fluffy white towels, the thermostat turned up a notch or two and a large bowl overflowing with different types of sponges, soaps and oils.

✳ As we've already seen, being able to block out the sun and dim the lights adds to the spa experience (see page 270), as do those extra little touches – towelling slippers and a luxury robe.

✳ If there's room, have a comfortable chair in the bathroom to relax in after you come out of the bath and use a fabulous scented linen spray on your towels.

GETTING IT READY FOR VISITORS

✳ Give the bathroom a thorough clean and then stow away any unsightly products – nobody needs to know what it takes to keep you looking good.

✳ Put out a little bowl or small tray with all the essentials your visitors might need (soap, toothpaste, a spare toothbrush etc.) – there's always someone who forgets something.

✳ When you're throwing a large party, direct visitors to the bathroom with a simple sign at the bottom of the stairs, plus a sign on the bathroom door to show that they've found the right room.

✳ If possible, don't have a hot shower just before your guests arrive. Give the bathroom a chance to dry out before visitors use it.

✳ Make it clear which towels are for guests' use by clearing away the family towels and put out some fresh guest towels (slightly smaller than hand towel size).

✳ Unwrap a new soap; it's ungenerous to be down to a slither.

✳ Spritz the room with a room fragrance and leave it on show so guests can use it if they want to.

✳ Add a little posy of flowers too – it shows you've made the effort.

*It's all the little indulgences that make a home spa experience feel special. For the price of one or two professional spa treatments you'll be able to buy all the kit to do it properly yourself; a new dressing gown and slippers, a pile of fluffy towels and a generous bowl full of all your favourite brushes, salts and soaps.

Make your own herb bath

The foliage of aromatic herbal plants such as rosemary, lavender, eucalyptus and lemon balm release their fragrant oils when gently crushed. Make yourself an aromatic herb bath by simply tying a bunch of leaves together, rubbing them between your fingers, then tying the bunch to the hot tap so it's in the stream of water.

Why it works:
The luxury ensuite

So many of us have sliced off a part of a bedroom to create a shower room or sacrificed the box room in order to give ourselves the luxury of our own bathing space, but there's also the option of putting the bath in your bedroom. Dream a little....

A bath in the bedroom

✳ It's perfectly feasible to install a bath within a reasonably sized bedroom, as it's not that difficult to extend the plumbing from an existing bathroom elsewhere in the home.

✳ Choose a bath you love – it will be a focal point of the room.

✳ Think about storage right from the start. A small table beside the bath will be enough for a few bottles of bath oil, soaps or a glass of wine. A nearby cupboard can be used to house towels.

✳ You'll also need a supersized floor mat to catch splashes.

THE DRESSING AREA

Neither the bathroom nor the dressing area takes over in this dual-function room. None of the clutter of the dressing area can be viewed whilst bathing. The aged finish on the bath means it fades into the background and almost looks like a piece of furniture rather than a bath.

ROOM FOR TWO

A double ended bath with taps mounted in the middle means there's comfortably room for two. Avoid shower attachments – they are too risky in a bedroom environment.

THE FEEL

Function is replaced with luxury. This room doesn't feel like a 'bathroom'. Practicality isn't at the forefront of its design. Imagine taking a bath here by candlelight with a lighted fire in the grate....

THE LIGHT

The folding screen at the window provides privacy during the day while still allowing plenty of light to flood in. It also adds another decorative layer to the room. The integral wooden shutters give complete privacy when needed. Spots in the ceiling are on dimmers, to provide subtle lighting during the evening.

THE PRACTICALITIES

Putting a bath in a large room like this, with high ceilings and windows that open easily, means there shouldn't be problems with damp. It would be a different story if you were using it for power showers each morning.

THE FURNITURE

Accessories and furniture – a luxury wool rug, a coffee table, a pair of chairs to invite bathside chats – are all unexpected in a 'bathroom'.

Children in the bathroom

'Kiddifying' a bathroom doesn't have to mean going to the extreme of installing child-sized fittings. Focus on items that can be easily be replaced and updated as the child grows.

SAFETY MATTERS
Safety comes first. Take expert advice about making the bathroom a safe place for small children. As well as fitting locks and safety catches to medicine cabinets, cupboards and the toilet seat, think about fitting a lock high up on the outside of the bathroom door. It will stop small children entering when you aren't there to supervise.

PUT IT AWAY
The toys, bubble baths, oils and creams will all need a home if the bathroom is to feel organised and stay uncluttered. Hooks and rails are ideal for storing dressing gowns, towels and bags of toys. It's also handy to have a laundry basket in the bathroom – it'll help your children get into the habit of dealing with their own dirty clothes.

EASY ACCESS
Make the things you do want the kids to reach easy for them to access. A step stool at the sink and the loo will help. Position storage low enough that they can reach it.

GETTING COLOURFUL
Bring in some colour, either by giving the walls a fresh coat of paint or with soft furnishings such as towels, cotton rugs (that can easily be thrown in the washing machine) and a blind or curtain.

WHAT'S MINE'S MINE
If you've got more than one child, help them keep track of their belongings. Sew an appliqué letter or monogram on their towels or a different coloured ribbon onto each child's towel. You could also give each child his or her own bathroom storage space (a hook with a monogramme or a colour-specific gym bag) to encourage them to put their kit away themselves.

*A stool or pouffe – ideally a towelling one – is useful for smaller children to use after a bath (see left) and gives adults something to perch on whilst the young ones bathe. Plastic buckets, or wicker baskets (see above) are a practical solution for bathtime paraphernalia. Giving each child designated storage – even if it's just colour-coded beakers will help prevent a jumble.

The wc and downstairs loo

This is one place where you can go a little crazy with the décor. It's an opportunity to show off and do something a bit quirky. If you've always loved a particularly mad colour, pattern or texture, this is the room to use it in. With such a small space, anything goes.

*Fit shelves for books or the overflow from other areas in the house, especially more decorative items like vases. Or hang artwork to create a mini gallery space – people often like having funny things to read on the walls.

Making the most of the smallest room in the house

✳ Get the basics covered first. Make sure that you're making the most of the (usually) small space so that it functions well.

✳ Task lighting isn't such a big consideration here. Visitors may be touching-up their make-up, but you don't need a full on bathroom lighting scheme.

✳ Don't be afraid to really go for it with the décor. It's the one room where you won't be judged – it's not too serious. Use bold patterned paper on all four walls or a vivid colour you wouldn't dream of using elsewhere.

✳ In a small area like this, it's easy to fragrance the space. Even an unlit scented candle will send out its aroma. But don't overdo it. This isn't the place for heady scents.

INDEX

INDEX

INDEX

INDEX

INDEX

ACKNOWLEDGEMENTS

Picture credits

Photographs by Clare Nolan other than those stated below.

b = bottom   t = top   l = left   r = right   f = far   m = middle

2: Brent Darby. 10:b: Sharon Ewer. 12, 14: Brent Darby. 16: tl: Lisa Cohen/Taverne; tr: Prue Ruscoe/Taverne; bl: Polly Eltes/Narratives; br: Marita Janssen/Taverne.
22: Nathalie Krag/Taverne Agency. 24/25: beachstudios.co.uk. 28: t: Lisa Cohen/Taverne Agency. 29: Prue Ruscoe/Taverne. 30: madeamano.com.
31: tl: Alun Callender/Narratives; tr: Polly Eltes/Narratives; m: mulberryhome.com; mr: crucial-trading.com; bl: Dan Duchars/Ideal Home/IPC. 34: br: Emma Lee/
Narratives. 35: tl: Kristin Perers/Associated News. 39: Polly Eltes/Narratives. 40/41: Brent Darby. 42, 43 tl: Rachel Whiting (styled by Stephanie Bateman Sweet);
43 br: Kristin Perers/Associated News. 44/45: Brent Darby. 46: Alun Callender/Narratives. 50: bl: Sharon Ewer; tm: thefrenchhouse.co.uk. 53: Haymarket Hotel
(designed by Kit Kemp). 54/55: Brent Darby. 57: Ingrid Rasmussen. 58: l: Polly Wreford (styled by Melanie Molesworth); right: argos.co.uk. 62/63 tl, inset
r: Tom Leighton/Associated News. 64: Paul Massey (home of Ben de Lisi). 65: l: Polly Eltes/Narratives; tr: Jan Baldwin/Narratives; br: Mikkel Vang/Taverne.
66: bl: Kristin Perers/Associated News; tr: home of laetitiamaklouf.com. 68/69: l: home of nathalie-lete.com; r: Alun Callender/Narratives (home of maggiealderson.
com). 70/71: Jake Curtis/Living Etc/IPC. 72: Simon Brown (home of Amy Somerville of somervillescott.com). 73: t: Brent Darby/Narratives; bl, Simon Brown (home
of Amy Somerville); br: Brent Darby (designed by sarahstewartsmith). 74: Ingrid Rasmussen/Associated News (home of nathalie-lete.com). 75: t: Ingrid Rasmussen;
b: Alun Callender (home of maggiealderson.com). 76: t: Tom Leighton/Associated News; 76 b, 78 t: Brent Darby/Associated News (designed by sarahstewartsmith.
com); 78b: Alun Callender/Narratives (home of Maggie Alderson). 80: t: Image Interiors/Narratives. 81: Alun Callender/ Narratives (home of josie-curran.com).
84: ml, mr: Ingrid Rasmussen. 86/87: Emma Lee/ Narratives. 90: Laura Edwards (studio of helenbeard.com). 91: thekitchendresser.co.uk. 94/95, 96/97, 100/101,
102/103: Brent Darby. 104: l: Ingrid Rasmussen; tr: Hilary Mandleberg. 105: tl: Hilary Mandleberg. 106/107: Birgitta Drejer/Sisters Agency. 108 br, 109: Ingrid Rasmussen. 114: tl: Polly Wreford/Navalis/Associated News; m: Chris Everard/Living etc/IPC. 115: tr: Sharon Ewer; bl: Polly Wreford/Navalis. 122: Polly Wreford/Narratives.
126/127: leefunnell.com. 129: tl: Brent Darby/Associated News. 130: Brent Darby. 142, 143: tm, br: Ingrid Rasmussen; bl: wildatheart.com 148: Sharon Ewer.
149 tl, br, 152 bl: Polly Wreford/Associated News. 153: Ingrid Rasmussen. 154: Robin Stubbert/Gap Interiors. 159: Rachel Whiting/Gap Interiors. 160: Brent
Darby(designed by sarahstewartsmith.com). 161: Douglas Gibb/Gap Interiors. 162: Ngoc Minh Ngo/Taverne. 164/165: bl: coxandcox.com; Adrian Briscoe (styled by
Melanie Molesworth). 166: tl: Redcover/Home Journal; tr: home of Kay and John Nolan; b: Simon Brown (home of Chrissie Probert Jones). 167: Rowland Roques
O Neil/Homes & Gardens/IPC. 168/169: Kristin Perers/Associated News. 170/171: Brent Darby (home of Kay and John Nolan). 173: Brent Darby (designed by
sarahstewartsmith.com). 176/177: Dana van Leeuwen/Taverne. 178/179: Marcus Peel. 180/181: Anouk de Kleermaeker/Taverne. 182/183: James Merrell/Living Etc/
IPC (home of Ben and Marina Fogle); bl: Mark Luscombe-Whyte/Homes & Gardens/IPC. 184: home of Bernadette and Andrew Harvey. 185: tr: Brent Darby
(home of Kay and John Nolan); bl: Brent Darby/Narratives; br: Emma Lee/Narratives (home of Jonathan Oliver). 186: l: Ngoc Minh Ngo/Taverne. 187: tl: Mikkel
Vang/Taverne; tr: Kristin Perers/Associated News. 189: Anouk de Kleermaeker/Taverne. 190/191: tl: Ed Reeve/Redcover; tr: Alexander James/Gap Interiors; bl: Henk
Brandsen/Taverne; br: Brent Darby (designed by sarahstewartsmith.com). 192/193: Polly Eltes/Narratives. 194/195, 198/199: plainenglishdesign.co.uk. 201: Claire
Richardson/Narratives. 202: Kristin Perers/Associated News. 203: tr: Paul Massey/Living Etc/IPC (home of Joanna Berryman, designed by matrushka.co.uk).
204: l: Simon Brown (home of Chrissie Probert Jones of stitchworks.com); r: Brent Darby/Narratives. 205: Alun Callender/Narratives. 206: tl, tr: Alun Callender/
Narratives; br: Holly Jolliffe/Narratives. 207: Jan Baldwin/Narratives. 209: Tessa Jol/Taverne Agency. 210: Ngoc Minh Ngo/Taverne. 211: Brent Darby.
212/213: Prue Ruscoe/Taverne. 220/221: Krisin Perers/Associated News. 223: Ngoc Minh Ngo/Taverne. 225: Brent Darby (designed by sarahstewartsmith.com).
226: Martin Hahn/Narratives. 228/229: l: Coco Amardeil/Camera Press. tr, br: Ingrid Rasmussen. 230: Brent Darby/Narratives. 231: Ingrid Rasmussen/Narratives.
232/233: Nathalie Krag/Taverne; bl: Polly Wreford/Homes & Gardens/IPC. 237: Mel Yates/Homes& Gardens/IPC. 238: Mikkel Vang/Taverne (designed by Kit
Kemp). 241: Rachel Whiting (styled by Laura Fulmine). 242/243: home of Bernadette and Andrew Harvey. 244: t: Brent Darby; b: Brent Darby/Narratives.
245: bl: Brent Darby; r: Nathalie Krag/Taverne. 247: tl: Brent Darby (designed by sarahstewartsmith.com). 248: Dana van Leeuwen/Taverne. 250: tl: niki-jones.co.uk;
tr: societylimonta.com; bl: lauraashley.com; br: Verity Welstead/Narratives. 251: m: niki-jones.co.uk; r: grahamandgreen.co.uk. 252/253: Prue Ruscoe/Taverne.
254: ml: Brent Darby. 256: t: Prue Ruscoe/Taverne Agency; b: Dana van Leeuwen/Taverne Agency. 257: John Dummer/Taverne Agency. 258: Alun Callender/
Narratives. 259: Emma Lee/Narratives. 261: Brent Darby/Narratives. 263: Polly Eltes/Narratives. 264: Holly Jolliffe/Narratives. 266: bl: Brent Darby; br: Jan Baldwin/
Narratives. 267: Visi/Greg Cox/ lifestylefeatures.com. 269: Mikkel Vang/Taverne. 271: Jon Day/Narratives. 272: bl: Brent Darby. 273: home of Kay and John Nolan.
274/275: Paul Massey/IPC (home of Joanna Berryman, designed by matrushka.co.uk); bl: Alun Callender/Narratives. 276: Reed Davis. 277: l: Polly Eltes/Narratives.
278: l: Dana van Leeuwen/Taverne; tr: John Dummer/Taverne; br: Ed Reeve/Redcover. 279: James Gardiner (home of supermarketsarah.com).

ACKNOWLEDGEMENTS

Sketchbook picture credits

b = bottom   t = top   l = left   r = right   f = far   m = middle

13: br: Simon Brown (home of suzihoodless.com). 14: br: scarletandviolet.com 15: tl: Ray Main/mainstreamimages.co.uk (home of Simon Young of re-foundobjects.com); bl: marksandspencer.com; br: re-foundobjects.com. 37: jar of buttons: coxandcox.co.uk. 60/61: patchwork sofa: squintlimited.com; fringed chair: thefrenchhouse.co.uk. 77: tl: Brent Darby/Associated News (designed by sarahstewartsmith.com); mfl: Trio Giovan/Gap Interiors; ml: Mikkel Vang/Taverne. 89: tl: therugcompany.info; chairs: Ingrid Rasmussen; china: Nato Welton. 128: crystal ball, animal lights: grahamandgreen.co.uk; chandeliers: thefrenchhouse.co.uk; bl: tomdixon.net; 163: tl: Simon Brown (home of suzihoodless.com); tm: Marcus Peel (home of Jonanna Berryman, designed by matrushka. co.uk); tr: Clive Nichols/Gap Interiors; bl: alternativeflooring.com; ml: Mel Yates/Red Cover; mr: Johnny Bouchier/Gap Interiors; br: Douglas Gibb/Gap interiors. 172: tl: Alun Callender (home of Rae Feather of thelondonfootstoolcompany.com); ml: Brent Darby (designed by sarahstewartsmith.com); mr: Costas Picadas/ Gap Interiors; br: Birgitta Drejer/Sisters Agency; 174: tl: the rugcompany.info; bl: Firmdale Hotels, designed by Kit Kemp; br: Mel Yates/grahamandgreen.co.uk; tr: Red Cover/Home Journal; 175: t: Nathalie Krag/Taverne; b: Brent Darby (designed by sarahstewartsmith.com); r: gpjbaker.com; 243: tl, bl, tr: Brent Darby; br: Jody Stewart (home of jen-jones.com); 249: tl: Ingrid Rasmussen/Associated News (home of interior designer Helen Green); tm: John Drummer/Taverne; bl: thewhitecompany.co.uk; 268: tl: Marcus Peel; bl: purlfrost.com; tm: Hotze Eisma/Taverne; bm: thenewenglandshuttercompany.com; mr: Marcus Peel (home of Joanna Berryman, designed by matrushka.co.uk); fr: madeamano.com.

Still-life credits

160: Chest of drawers and acrylic console: conranshop.com; round table: ikea.com. 170: top and second from bottom: georgesmith.com. 208: (from top): benchmarkfurniture.com; conranshop.com; ikea.com; helengreendesign.com, benchmarkfurniture.com. 210: (from top): benchmarkfurniture.com; thediningchair. co.uk; the diningchair.co.uk; conranshop.com; helengreendesign.com. 224: second from top: twentytwentyone.com; all others conranshop.com. 240: (from top to bottom): thewhitecompany.com; featherandblack.com; thefrenchbedroomcompany.co.uk; anthropologie.com; helengreendesign.com.

Suppliers

A big thank you goes to all the suppliers who so generously allowed me to reproduce their images (see above), loaned me product for shoots or didn't mind me snapping their gorgeous shops. This list pretty much reads as my little black book:

anthropologie.com	merci-merci.com
chloealberry.com	nicolefarhi.com
conranshop.co.uk	okadirect.com
designersguild.com	originalbtc.com
gardentrading.co.uk	osborneandlittle.com
grahamandgreen.co.uk	scarletandviolet.com
harrisandjones.co.uk	summerillandbishop.com
houseoffraser.co.uk	thefrenchhouse.co.uk
ianmankin.co.uk	therugcompany.com
juniorgeo.co.uk	thewhitecompany.com
johnlewis.com	united-perfumes.com
littlegreene.com	williamyeoward.com

AUTHOR ACKNOWLEDGEMENTS

Thanks to all the team at YOU magazine for their support and encouragement, especially Sue Peart, my Editor, for allowing me to take on this project alongside my role at YOU and for being 100 per cent behind me. I couldn't have wished for more.

-

Kyle Cathie for her unwavering confidence and enthusiasm in my ideas and saying yes in the first place. And her team, both in-house and out, especially Judith Hannam, Laura Foster and Hilary Mandleberg for their nerves of steel and stamina – it's been a huge challenge to produce such an expansive book together. Dale Walker, for doing such a superb layout – it has been a joy working with you. Nicole Gray, for the laughter and can-do approach whilst assisting me on some of the shoots. Brent Darby, Ingrid Rasmussen and Sharon Ewer for taking such wonderful pics when my own snappy snaps just didn't pass muster.

-

My family are amongst my best friends, and are a constant source of encouragement and support. Thanks to my sister Bernie and her husband Andrew Harvey; my sister-in-law Kay and John Nolan, and my dad, Michael Nolan, for letting me temporarily take over their houses on my shoots.

-

Thanks to all my friends for their absolute support and unflagging friendship. Jaqui Jeans-Lowry for teaching me the meaning of possibility and giving me the firm push that I needed. Sarah Stewart Smith and Juliette Tomlinson, for being there with me right from the very beginning and keeping me steady and sane along the way – your insight has been invaluable. Apologies go out to all my friends for disappearing off the radar and being even more of a recluse than usual, thanks for hanging in there.

-

This project is the culmination of nearly 15 years of working alongside some of the best talent in the lifestyle industry. I've been lucky enough to meet some of the most talented designers, makers and decorators and share their insight. These creatives, along with the stylists, photographers and writers who I've worked alongside, have inspired me most. Thank you for feeding my creativity – you have inspired me in ways you may never have imagined. I am very grateful for all the generosity of the suppliers who allowed me to use their photographs and products within the book (see opposite for credits).

-

And, finally, a special thanks to Jonathan, my husband-to-be, for keeping me fed and watered whilst I tap-tap-tapped this book out and his boundless patience as I turned our home upside down for yet another shoot. But most importantly for his unfailing support and faith in my dreams. Thank you for helping them materialise.

Clare Nolan has an innate and distinctive sense of style – her work is always thought-provoking and captures a relaxed and carefree spirit that enhances and enriches the way we decorate our homes today

Tricia Guild